*French Chic*

# EMBROIDERY

100 IDEES

BALLANTINE BOOKS · NEW YORK

*Contributing Editor:* Jan Eaton
*Art Editor:* Caroline Courtney
*Design Assistant:* Caroline Pickles
*Text Editor:* Mary Trewby
*Illustrators:* Prue Bucknell, Robina Green
Peter Meadows, Coral Mula,
Caroline Pickles, Cooper West

The DMC embroidery materials used in this book are
available in most large sewing stores. If not, you may
order them from:
American Needlewoman
3806 Alta Mesa Blvd.
Fort Worth, TX 76133

Conceived, designed and produced by
Conran Octopus Limited
28-32 Shelton Street
London WC2 9PH

Library of Congress Catalog Card Number: 85-91564

ISBN 0-345-33608-9

Manufactured in Hong Kong

First American Edition: August 1986

10 9 8 7 6 5 4 3 2 1

# CONTENTS

# INTRODUCTION

The decoration of fabric with thread has been practiced for centuries to create beautiful items, both functional and ornamental. The fascination of embroidery lies in the way complex and elaborate designs can be built up from simply worked stitches.

The designs in this book are suitable for the beginner and the experienced stitcher, ranging from easy-to-work strawberry and cherry motifs to the delightful floral spray shown on this page. In addition to embroidery on fabric, canvas work is also well represented by some stunning designs including tiny petit point purses and a bedcover featuring a countryside theme. Many of the larger canvas work projects are made less daunting by being worked in small sections which are easier to handle.

Select a design which is initially within your capabilities and gain experience in handling fabric and thread. Then move on to the more challenging projects when you feel confident with your technical skill. Always use the best fabric you can afford so the embroidery will give you pleasure for many years.

## THREADS

Embroidery threads are available in a wide range of weights and colors. The most common threads are cotton or wool, but pure silk, linen, synthetic and metallic threads can also be bought. Some threads are twisted and cannot be divided; while others are made up of several strands which can be separated to give a finer thread. The strands can be put together to give different weight and color combinations, or mixed with another thread.

The following threads are used in this book:
*Stranded cotton* a lustrous six-stranded thread which can be separated.
*Pearl cotton* a twisted, shiny thread which cannot be divided and is used as a single thread.
*Danish flower thread* a soft, fine linen thread.
*Tapestry wool* a twisted 4-ply pure wool thread which is hardwearing and mothproofed.
*Rug wool* a twisted heavyweight pure wool yarn used for either stitched or tufted rugs.

## FABRICS

There are three types of fabrics used for embroidery: plain-weave fabrics, even-weave fabrics and canvas. 'Plain-weave' is the term used to describe any woven fabric, regardless of fiber content. The outline of an embroidery design is usually transferred on to this type of fabric, to act as a guide during the stitching.

Even-weave fabrics, although also plain-weave, have an important difference in the construction of the weave. The warp and weft threads are of identical thickness and the weave of the fabric is perfectly regular. The same number of warp and weft threads occur in a given area, making a regular grid so that stitches can be worked accurately by counting the threads and following a chart. The even-weave fabric group also contains fabrics which have the threads woven together in pairs or in regular blocks – these fabrics are usually made of cotton and cotton blends.

Canvas is made from stiffened cotton warp and weft threads woven together to produce spaced holes between the threads, giving the fabric a regular grid-like structure. This grid is usually completely covered by the embroidery stitches, often worked from a chart. Canvas is available in different grid sizes (gauges), which indicate the number of threads which can be stitched in a 1 in (2.5cm) square. Single canvas has a single-thread grid, and double canvas has pairs of threads forming the grid.

## NEEDLES

Crewel, chenille and tapestry needles are the types of needles used for embroidery. They have larger eyes than ordinary sewing needles to accommodate a thicker thread.
*Crewel needles:* medium-length needles used for fine and medium-weight embroidery on plain-weave fabrics.
*Chenille needles:* are longer and thicker, and have larger eyes than crewel needles, which makes them suitable for use with heavier threads and fabrics.
*Tapestry needles:* similar in shape to chenille needles, but with a blunt end rather than a sharp point. They are used for embroidery on even-weave fabrics and canvas.

All needles are graded from fine to coarse, with the lower number denoting the coarser needles. Needle sizes are suggested in this book, but you may prefer to use a different size according to your personal preference.

## EMBROIDERY FRAMES

All embroidery will be more successful if the fabric or canvas is held taut in an embroidery frame. It is not only easier to handle, but the stitches will be more regular and distortion of the fabric is kept to a minimum. There are several types of frame available, and the choice depends on the fabric, the size of the project and your own preference. A simple round frame or hoop is suitable for embroidery on plain-weave fabrics. If the project is quite large, the hoop can be quickly and easily moved along the fabric after a portion of the stitching has been completed. Canvas should be stretched in a rectangular frame, large enough to accommodate the whole piece. The simplest rectangular frame is a wooden stretcher to which the canvas is attached by thumb tacks or staples. You can make a frame from four wooden stretchers joined at the corners. They are available in a wide range of sizes in art stores. Specialist embroidery frames (square or rotating frames) are adjustable and stretch the fabric very evenly. A hoop or a rectangular frame can be used with even-weave fabric, depending on the size of the project.

## ENLARGING A DESIGN

Enlarging the designs in this book to the correct size is not difficult to do successfully, but accurate measuring is important. Basically, the technique consists of dividing the original design into equal squares and then carefully copying the design, square for square, on to a larger grid. First trace the design from the book on to a piece of tracing paper, centering it; then follow the diagrams shown on this page. The most accurate way to copy the image is to mark each place where the design lines cross the larger grid, and then join up these marks.

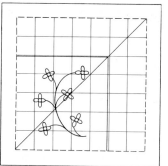

1. *Draw a grid square over the trace, and then draw in a diagonal. Using this line as a guide, grid in the whole of the larger piece of paper.*

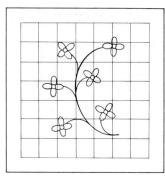

2. Once the entire pattern has been transferred on to the larger grid, check it back very carefully against the original pattern.

## TRANSFERRING A DESIGN

When the design has been enlarged to the correct size, you will need to transfer it on to the fabric before the embroidery is begun.

Four transfer methods are shown here:
*Carbon paper:* works well on most fabrics and is quick and easy. Use dressmakers' carbon paper, which is available in different colors rather than the type sold by a stationer.
*Transfer pencil:* gives a result similar to a commercial transfer. Always match the iron temperature to the composition of the fabric.
*Pricking and pouncing:* a traditional method which is time-consuming but gives a very accurate copy. Use this method in preference to the first two when the fabric is delicate and the design is detailed and intricate.

*Using a light source:* will give a very accurate copy, but can only be used when the fabric is finely woven and is a pale color.

## EMBROIDERY STITCHES

The stitches used on the projects are shown below, and they are all quite simple to work. With some of the stitches such as satin stitch and long and short stitch, practice will be needed to work

them neatly and get good fabric coverage. Follow the diagrams carefully if the stitch is one you are not familiar with.

Work with the fabric or canvas stretched in an embroidery hoop or frame as this will help you to keep the stitches regular, and

remember not to pull the threads too tightly. The individual instructions will give you details of how to work the designs, where to start stitching, how many strands of thread to use, and suggested needle sizes.

Do not use a knot on the back

of the fabric or canvas as an unsightly bulge will appear on the right side. Instead, leave a short length of thread hanging, use the needleful of thread and then carefully secure both the ends on the wrong side by threading them through the stitches.

*straight stitch*

*feather stitch*

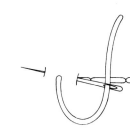

*back stitch*

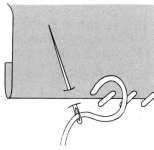

*hemming stitch*

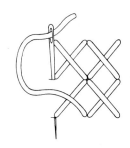

*cross stitch*

*chain stitch*

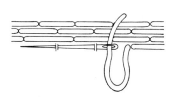

*darning stitch*

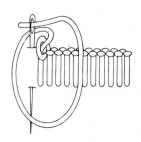

*buttonhole stitch*

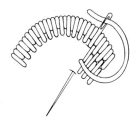

*long and short stitch*

*satin stitch*

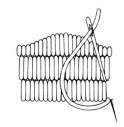

*encroaching satin stitch*

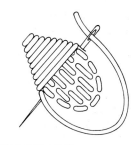

*padded satin stitch*

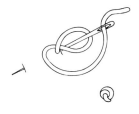

*Chinese knots*

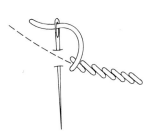

*stem stitch*

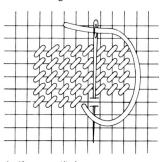

*half cross stitch*

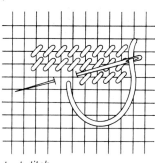

*tent stitch*

# STRAWBERRY FAIR

Tendrils of wild strawberries make a perfect border for a white tablecloth, set for summer. They have the restrained prettiness of an Edwardian, hand-painted watercolor. Chinese knots are used for the berry seeds over satin stitch, in subtle blends of color.

## MATERIALS

One plain white tablecloth with a fine, smooth weave, preferably in pure cotton. If a square cloth is used it should measure at least 5ft 6in (165cm) across to allow for one complete spray to be worked along each side. If you prefer a rectangular cloth, the length should be at least 4ft 6in (137cm) to accommodate one complete spray along each long side. Crewel needle size 7 or 8. Embroidery hoop

**Threads**
DMC stranded cotton
Flowers: **pink** 819, 3689; **gold** 676; **green** 954
Strawberries: **red** 321, 498, 815; **white**
LEAVES 1: **green** 367, 989; veins – **green** 319
LEAVES 2: **gold** 834; **green** 3013; veins – **dull green** 3053

**Embroidery Stitches**
Long and short stitch, encroaching satin stitch, satin stitch, Chinese knots, stem stitch.

## DIRECTIONS

▦ Enlarge the design on page 10 to the measurements given on the pattern. Transfer it to the cloth using one of the methods given on page 6.

▦ Work with the cloth stretched in an embroidery hoop, moving the hoop along the cloth as each portion is completed, and use three strands of the thread.

▦ To embroider the flowers, work one row of long and short stitch in the deep pink along the edge of the petals. Fill in the petals using the light pink and the same stitch until the center circle is reached.

▦ Mass Chinese knots in yellow to make the raised center and work the small leaves between the petals in green satin stitch.

▦ Embroider the strawberries in encroaching satin stitch in three shades of red: use the darkest red to outline the shape, and then fill in towards the center, shading the fruit from dark to light.

▦ Scatter tiny white Chinese knots over this stitching.

▦ Work the calyx in satin stitch using either green or gold, as shown on the pattern.

▦ Embroider the leaves in shades of green (leaves 1) or gold (leaves 2), as indicated on the pattern. Work a row of encroaching satin stitch in the darker color round the edge of the leaf and then fill in the remainder using the same stitch and the lighter color.

▦ Work the veins in stem stitch.

▦ Embroider the stalks in stem stitch using one strand of each green used on leaf 1 to make up a three-strand thread.

▦ When the embroidery is complete, place the cloth face down on a well-padded surface and press lightly, taking care not to crush the stitches.

*The flower and strawberry are shown life-size. Use them as a guide for blending the colors from dark to light. They also show the stitches which are used for each motif.*

# delicious berries for summer settings

*Use the leaf diagrams as a guide to blending the different colors of encroaching satin stitch. Leaf 1 is in three shades of green and leaf 2 is in green mixed with gold*

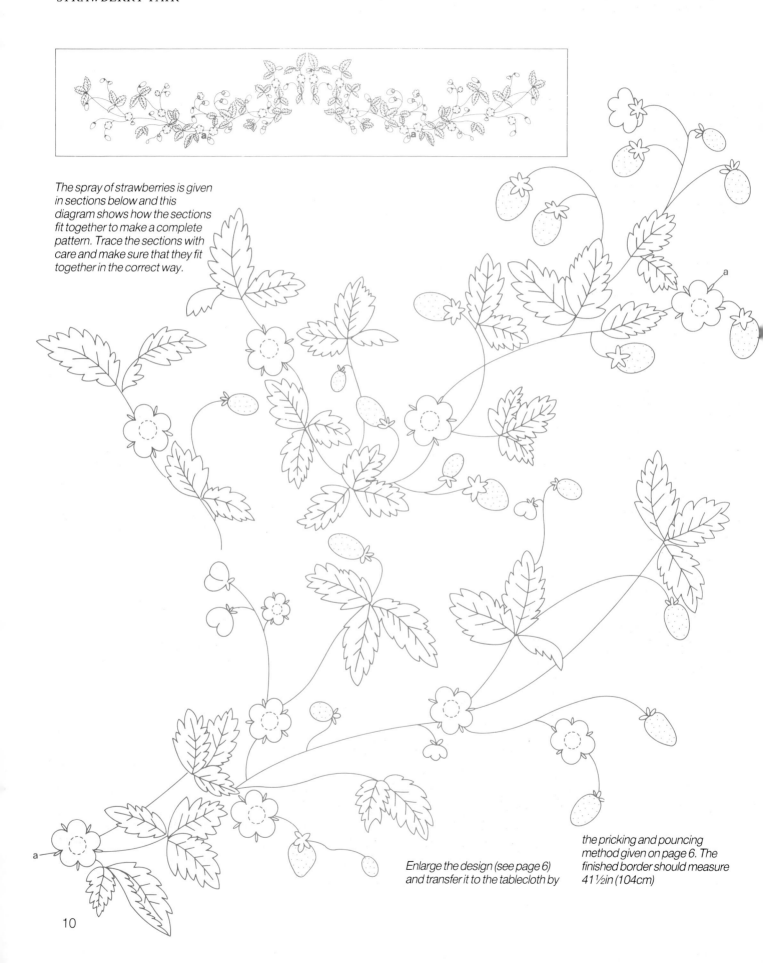

The spray of strawberries is given in sections below and this diagram shows how the sections fit together to make a complete pattern. Trace the sections with care and make sure that they fit together in the correct way.

Enlarge the design (see page 6) and transfer it to the tablecloth by the pricking and pouncing method given on page 6. The finished border should measure 41½in (104cm)

10

# T-SHIRT GRAFFITI

## MATERIALS

| | |
|---|---|
| One white T-shirt | Crewel needle size 7 or 8 |

**Threads**
*DMC stranded cotton:*
*2 strands of* **black** *310*
*1 strand each of:*
**yellow** *727, 783, 972, 973;* **red**
*666;* **rose pink** *602, 962, 963;*
**blue** *794, 799, 996;* **green** *368,*
*701*

**Embroidery Stitches**
*stem stitch, satin stitch, infilling*
*chain stitch.*

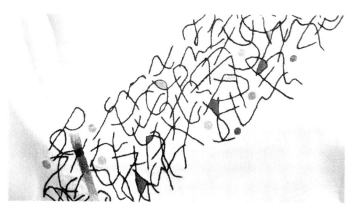

## DIRECTIONS

▦ Lay the T-shirt on a flat surface and mark out the area for the embroidery: Mark a 4-5in (10-13cm) wide strip from one base corner across the front to the opposite shoulder and down the sleeve with basting stitches. Using a light marking pen or pencil fill in between the tacked lines with interlocking letters and scribbles, following the picture and overlapping the tacked lines at intervals to produce an uneven edge.

▦ Using black embroidery cotton, work over the lines in stem stitch. Fill in the small enclosed sections of the design using different colors in satin stitch. Add small circles of color in infilling chain stitch at spaced intervals and, to complete the design, two bands of satin stitch in graduating colors.

▦ When the embroidery is completed, place it face down on a well-padded surface and press lightly, taking care not to crush the stitches.

# ETHNIC FLOWERS

The brilliant colors of Hungarian floral embroidery have a timeless attraction. The beauty of these flowers is that you can be as ambitious or as small-scale as you like: a plain white dress can be made into a treasured object, or the motifs can be embroidered singly or in clusters for a bag, the front edges of a blouse, for the corner of a shawl or the point of a collar. And they are done simply and quickly in satin stitch and stem stitch. Vary the flower colors to your own taste, but keep them jewel-bright. As with the genuine article, a certain roughness in technique adds life.

## MATERIALS

A ready-made garment, or fabric to be made into a shawl, tablecloth or cushion cover.

Crewel needle size 5 or 6
Embroidery hoop

**Threads**
DMC cotton perle no. 8 in the following shades:
SOLID COLORS: **green** 703, 704, 895; **yellow** 745, 973; **pink** 352, 818; **orange** 971; **red** 349, 606, 608, 817; **dark red** 815, 902, 3685; **purple** 550
SHADED COLOURS: **green** 122, 126; **blue** 113; **orange** 108; **pink** 99, 112; **red** 57; **mauve** 126

**Embroidery Stitches**
Satin stitch, stem stitch.

## DIRECTIONS

▦ Transfer the chosen motifs to the fabric or garment using either the carbon paper method or the transfer pencil method given on page 6.
▦ Work with the fabric or garment stretched in an embroidery hoop, moving the hoop as necessary. If the fabric is very fine or delicate, protect it from damage with a piece of muslin (see page 6).
▦ Using the photograph and diagram on page 14 as color guides, embroider the flowers and leaves in satin stitch and the stems in stem stitch.
▦ When the embroidery is completed, place it face down on a well-padded surface and press lightly, taking care not to crush the stitches.

# the richness of a folk tradition

The flower motifs can be used to decorate other objects: a box lid (see page 22) or a handkerchief. Embroider some of the larger motifs on to a piece of satin and use the instructions on page 76 to make an elegant purse.

The floral designs are intended to be used in an individual way. Be as creative as you like: select single motifs and scatter them over the fabric; mass the flowers closely together to create the riot of color shown on the previous page; use use just one motif to highlight a garment.

# CHORISTERS' COLLARS

These pretty collars in simple cross stitch are detachable, so they can be washed easily and worn with a variety of outfits. By choosing harmonious colors – gray and yellow, pink and blue, green and turquoise – you can make them to match any favorite dress or smock.

## MATERIALS

| | |
|---|---|
| For each design: | Crewel needle size 7 or 8 |
| 12in (30cm) × 15in (38cm) even-weave 18-gauge fabric, in white | Sewing needle |
| | 5 pairs of small snap fasteners |
| White sewing thread | 1yd (1m) white cotton bias binding |

### Threads
DMC stranded cotton:
1 strand of each: **yellow** 445; **gray** 318

### Embroidery Stitch
Cross stitch: each square on the charts represents one cross stitch worked over two horizontal and two vertical woven blocks of the fabric.

## DIRECTIONS

▦ Enlarge the collar pattern to full size on plain paper from the measurements given (see page 6). Check the neckline of the dress to which the collar is to be attached against that of the pattern; adjust if necessary.

▦ Pin the pattern to the fabric and cut out the collar.

▦ Bind the neck edge of the collar with bias binding, as shown in the diagram. Then turn a double ⅜in (1cm) hem around the remaining edges (see page 79 for instructions on mitering corners), pin and hand stitch. Press.

▦ Beginning ⅝in (2cm) above the hem and working from the center front outwards, embroider the chosen design from the chart in cross stitch. Use three strands of thread throughout.

▦ When the embroidery is completed, place it face down on a well-padded surface and press lightly, taking care not to crush the stitches.

▦ Sew snap fasteners to the collar and dress, placing one pair of snaps at the center fronts, one on each shoulder line, and one at each side of the center-back opening.

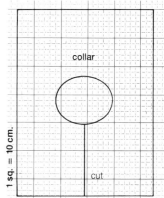

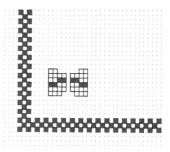

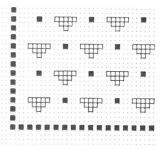

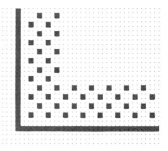

# BEETLE BACKS

Little monsters with shiny exotic wings are a wittier decoration to wear on your sleeve than a tender heart! They look all the better for advancing in a cluster: simple satin and straight stitch make them easy to embroider. The designs were copied straight from a book on insects – why not explore studies on fauna for some other unusual motifs? With luck you can find a subject just the right size and trace directly over it for your transfer.

## MATERIALS

| | |
|---|---|
| Ready-made white cotton shirt with short sleeves | Small piece of stiff card |
| Crewel needle size 7 or 8 | Embroidery hoop |

**Threads**
DMC stranded cotton as indicated below each beetle.

**Embroidery Stitches**
Satin stitch, straight stitch.

## DIRECTIONS

 Enlarge the designs to the desired dimension. Place the piece of card in the sleeve to protect the under-sleeve and transfer the design to the fabric using the carbon paper method given on page 6. Then remove the card.

 Work with the fabric stretched in an embroidery hoop, moving the hoop as necessary.

 Using the photographs and diagrams as color guides, embroider each beetle body in satin stitch and the antennae and narrow parts of the legs in straight stitch. Use two strands of threads throughout.

 When the embroidery is completed, place it face down on a well-padded surface and press lightly, taking care not to crush the stitches.

BEETLE 1: **yellow** 742, 747; **green** 943, 991; **blue** 807

BEETLE 2: **yellow** 307, 726; **ocher** 783; **brown** 434; **black** 310

BEETLE 3: **red** 355; **green** 943, 991; **brown** 301; **ocher** 783

BEETLE 4: **green** 704, 943, 991; **yellow** 727; **brown** 801

BEETLE 5: **yellow** 744, 783; **black** 310; **chestnut** 976

BEETLE 6: **yellow** 472; **black** 310; **ocher** 729

BEETLE 7: **red** 666; **black** 310; **yellow** 727

BEETLE 8: **orange** 741; **brown** 3371; **red** 349; **ocher** 729

*a surprise from nature's sketch-book*

# PERENNIAL PLEASURES

This rich anemone spray adds individuality and color to a simple classic sweater. Much easier to achieve than it at first appears, the embroidery is worked on a small piece of fine cotton and then appliquéd on to the sweater in a cunning method that makes the joining invisible. You could stitch a floral spray like this – perhaps scaled down – to attach to a velvet or silk cummerbund, to the back of a kimono or a light jacket.

## MATERIALS

Ready-made round-necked cotton sweater in pink (the sweater should be of a medium weight to support the embroidery adequately).

16in (40cm) × 12in (30cm) fine white cotton fabric.
Crewel needle size 4 or 5
Embroidery hoop

### Threads
DMC stranded cotton:
2 skeins of each of the following colors: SOLID COLORS: **pink** 600, 601, 602, 603, 604, 605, 754, 818, 819, 948; **yellow** 3078; **green** 320, 730, 734; **red** 606, 666, 815; **blue** 793; **mauve** 554
SHADED COLORS: **blue** 67, 121, 124; **pink** 48, 62, 112; **mauve** 52, 95, 99, 126; **green** 92, 94

### Embroidery Stitch
Long and short stitch with a stitch length of approximately ⅛ to ³⁄₁₆in (3 to 4mm).

## DIRECTIONS

▦ Enlarge the design to the measurements given on the pattern (see page 6). Transfer the design to the fine white cotton using one of the methods given on page 6.

▦ Work with the fabric stretched in an embroidery hoop, moving the hoop as necessary.

▦ Using the photograph and diagram as color guides, embroider the flowers and leaves in long and short stitch, but leave a narrow area the width of one row of stitches inside the edge of the design. Work with six strands of thread throughout.

▦ When the embroidery is completed apart from the border strip, place it face down on a well-padded surface and press lightly, taking care not to crush the stitches.

▦ Cut away the surplus fabric with a sharp pair of scissors.

▦ Tack the embroidery in place on the sweater. Then work the border strip in long and short stitch, taking the stitches through both the fabric and the jumper and keeping them close together so that the fabric edge is completely covered.

Place the embroidery over the right shoulder as shown.

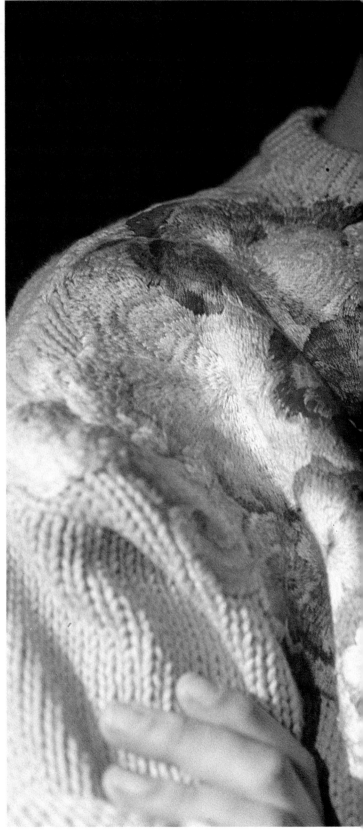

# *cut flowers that last . . .*

To make the belt shown in the picture above, cut a length of belt stiffening to the correct size and place centrally to the wrong side of the embroidery. Fold the edges of the embroidered fabric over the stiffening, making neat corners. Cut a length of lining to the correct size plus ⅝in (1.5cm) all round. Turn in all edges and handstitch to wrong side of belt. Handstitch ribbon centrally to right side.

The design overlaps by ⅜in (1cm) at the center. Trace the two sections and overlap the tracings to get the complete pattern.

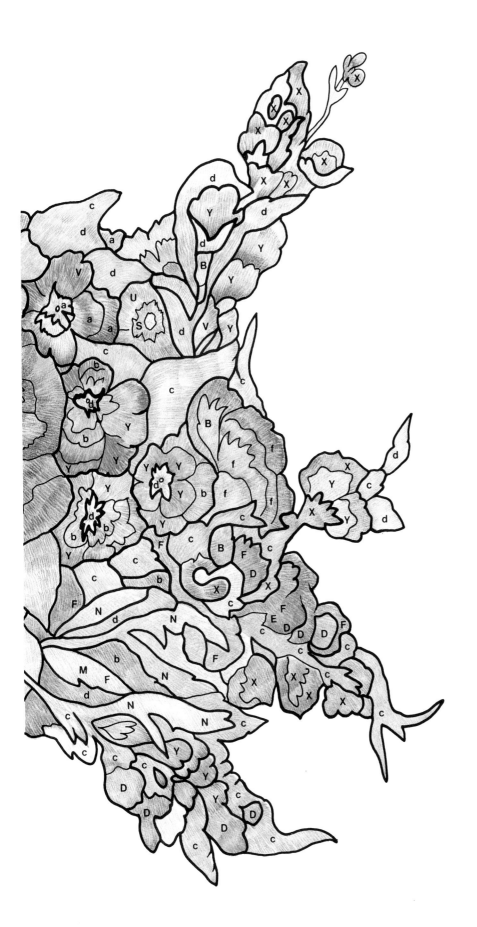

**KEY**

| | |
|---|---|
| A | 600 |
| B | 601 |
| C | 602 |
| D | 603 |
| E | 604 |
| F | 605 |
| G | 754 |
| H | 818 |
| I | 819 |
| J | 948 |
| K | 3078 |
| L | 320 |
| M | 730 |
| N | 734 |
| P | 666 |
| Q | 815 |
| R | 793 |
| S | 554 |
| T | 67 |
| U | 121 |
| V | 124 |
| W | 48 |
| X | 62 |
| Y | 112 |
| Z | 107 |
| a | 52 |
| b | 126 |
| c | 92 |
| d | 94 |
| e | 95 |
| f | 106 |
| g | 606 |
| h | 99 |

*The thicker outlines on the design indicate the main shapes, with the thin lines detailing the shading of the interlocking long and short stitches.*

*The colored areas on the design will act as a guide to the threads, but refer to the key shown above for the accurate thread numbers.*

# PROVENÇAL PRINTS

These flowered objects were inspired by the traditional fabrics of Provence. Use the violets to decorate a fabric-covered box, a letter file or a jewel case. The tiny swags look particularly fine on a typical abstract French print. Satin stitch and stem stitch in faded colored silks give the fresh-washed, sun-bleached character of the original textile designs.

## MATERIALS

SMALL BOX:

Flattish cardboard box with a
   hinged lid
Cotton fabric with a small
   geometric design
Crewel needle size 7 or 8
Embroidery hoop

LARGE BOX:

Cardboard box with a lid
Cotton fabric with a large floral
   design
Cotton fabric with a small
   geometric design
Crewel needle size 7 or 8
Embroidery hoop

**Threads**
DMC stranded cotton:
1 skein in each of the following
colors:
**yellow** 677, 745, 746; **green**
502, 503; **blue** 930, 931; **pink**
961; **black** 310

**Threads:** DMC stranded cotton
in colors to match the fabric

**Embroidery Stitches**
Long and short stitch, satin
stitch, stem stitch.

## DIRECTIONS

FOR THE SMALL BOX:
▦ Cut a piece of geometrically patterned fabric to fit the box lid, allowing a margin of 2in (5cm) all round. Enlarge the design to fit across the lid (see page 6).
▦ Transfer the design to the fabric using one of the methods given on page 6.
▦ Work with the fabric stretched in an embroidery hoop, moving the hoop as necessary.
▦ Using the diagram as a color guide, embroider the design in long and short stitch with two strands of thread.

FOR THE LARGE BOX:
▦ Cut a piece of the floral fabric to fit the lid, allowing a margin of 2in (5cm) all round and positioning one or two of the floral sprays attractively on the top of the lid.
▦ Work with the fabric stretched in an embroidery hoop, moving the hoop as necessary.
▦ Using the close-up photograph as a stitch guide,

embroider over the flowers and leaves: use long and short stitch for the petals and leaves, pick out tiny areas of color in satin stitch and work the stems and outlines in stem stitch. Use two strands of thread in matching colors throughout.

TO MAKE UP THE BOXES:
▦ Place the embroidery face down on a well-padded surface and press lightly, taking care not to crush the stitches.
▦ Trim the margins to ¾in (2cm) and follow the instructions shown in the diagrams for covering the boxes.

*Trace pattern for the small box.*

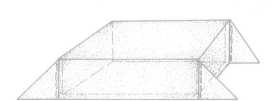

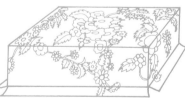

Place the fabric over the box with wrong sides outside. Pin out excess fabric equally at each corner in line with box corners. Remove fabric and stitch each corner level with box edge. Trim off excess fabric and press seam open. Replace over box and glue in place. Fold excess fabric to inside and glue.

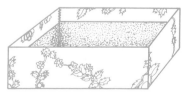

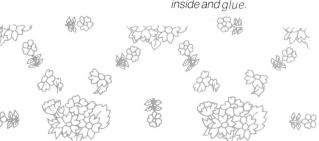

*imitate the patterns of France*

# LEMON AND LIME SQUARES

Cross stitch is easy to follow and satisfyingly simple to do well, but you need not limit yourself to squared canvas if you enjoy this embroidery. The lemons and leaves are stitched through canvas which provides an easy-to-use grid on a fine-weave white, ready-made tablecloth. The lime and leaf-green cross-stitched overcloth is made by joining embroidered squares with herringbone stitches. There's a variety of designs, offering you all kinds of different settings.

## MATERIALS FOR TABLECLOTH

| | |
|---|---|
| *Ready-made white cotton or linen tablecloth, approximately 6ft (1.8m) × 6ft 6in (2m)* | *8 pieces of single-thread 12-gauge canvas, each 6in (15cm) × 7in (18cm)*<br>*Crewel needle size 5 or 6* |

**Threads**
*DMC stranded cotton in the following colors:*
*6 skeins of **green** 701, 895; 5 skeins of **yellow** 445; 4 skeins of **yellow** 444, 972; 3 skeins of **green** 987; 3 skeins of **cream** 746*

**Embroidery Stitch**
*Cross stitch: each square on the chart represents one cross stitch worked over one vertical and one horizontal canvas thread.*

## DIRECTIONS FOR TABLECLOTH

▦ Each piece of canvas is slightly larger than the lemon motif, providing a regular grid on which to work the cross stitch lemons.
▦ Tack the rectangles of canvas to the tablecloth, positioning them as shown in the photograph with two lemon motifs at each corner of the cloth.
▦ Embroider the design carefully following the chart. Stitch base cloth, using six strands of thread.
▦ When the embroidery is completed, carefully cut away the surplus canvas close to the stitching. Gently pull out the remaining canvas threads from beneath the stitching with a pair of tweezers: avoid snagging.
▦ Place the cloth face down on a well-padded surface and press lightly, taking care not to crush the stitches.

*Place the motifs at each corner.*

*fresh colors for alfresco tables*

## MATERIALS FOR OVERCLOTH

6 squares of white even-weave 12-gauge fabric, each 14in (35cm) × 14in (35cm)

Crewel needle size 7 or 8
Crewel needle size 4 or 5
White sewing thread

### Threads
DMC stranded cotton: 4 skeins of each of the following colors: design 1 **green** 989, 3348; design 2 **green** 580, 909; design 3 **green** 3348, **kingfisher blue** 996; design 4 **green** 986, 988; design 5 **green** 701, 704; design 6 **green** 701, 895; plus 4 skeins of **green** 701 for joining the squares

### Embroidery Stitches
Cross stitch for working the designs: one square on the chart represents one cross stitch worked over one woven block of the fabric; feather stitch for joining the squares.

## DIRECTIONS

▦ Run a vertical and a horizontal line of guide basting through the center of each square of fabric to correspond with the center lines on the charts.
▦ Embroider the designs from the charts, working from the center outwards. Use three strands of thread and the finer crewel needle throughout.
▦ Repeat the patterns on the charts until each area of embroidery measures 12in (30cm) × 12in (30cm).

▦ Turn a double ⅜in (1cm) hem all round each square (see page 79 for instructions on mitering the corners) and hand stitch with white thread.
▦ When the squares are completed, place them face down on a well-padded surface and press lightly, taking care not to crush the stitches.
▦ Join the squares edge to edge, as shown in the diagram, by working a row of feather stitch with six strands of green 701 thread and the larger crewel needle. Press the joinings lightly.

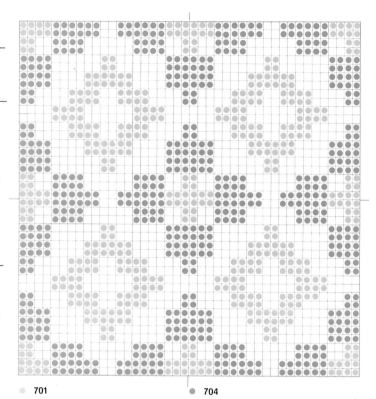

701          704

The overcloth is made up of these six different cross stitch squares.

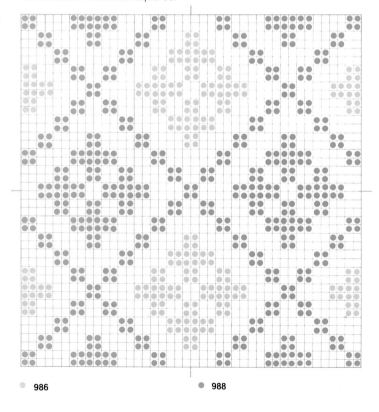

986          988

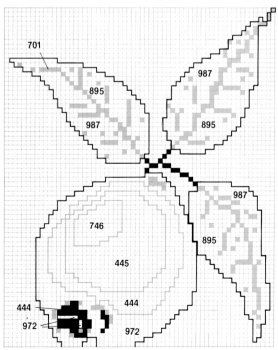

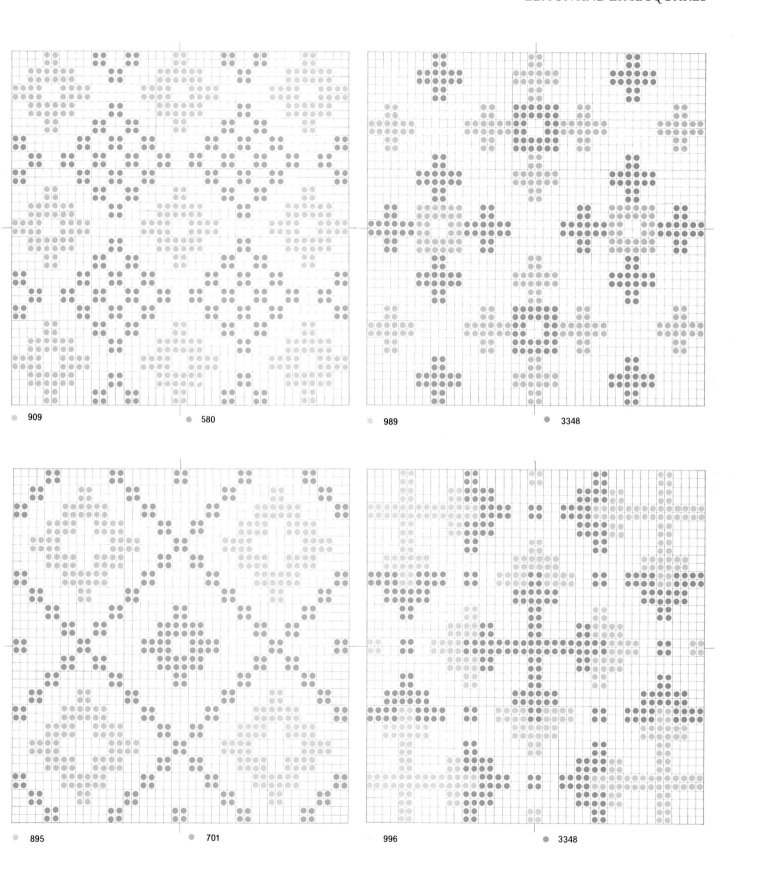

909   580

989   3348

895   701

996   3348

# JUICY FRUITS

Clusters of strawberries or cherries are a perfect decoration for summer whites and pastels – for a dress yoke, a pretty sash or bow, for collars, cuffs, and hemlines. Satin stitch and Chinese knots are quick to embroider and brighten up all sorts of modest everyday objects, such as a tablecloth and napkins or plain kitchen curtains.

## MATERIALS

| | |
|---|---|
| Ribbon and ready-made garment, or household linen | Crewel needle size 4 or 5<br>Embroidery hoop |

| **Threads** | **Embroidery Stitches** |
|---|---|
| DMC stranded cotton:<br>THE STRAWBERRIES: **red** 309;<br>**green** 911, 954<br>THE CHERRIES: **red** 321; **green** 909 | Satin stitch, Chinese knots. |

## DIRECTIONS

▦ Transfer the design to the fabric using one of the methods given on page 6.

▦ Work with the fabric stretched in an embroidery hoop.

▦ Embroider the strawberries and leaves in satin stitch using the red and darker green threads, then scatter Chinese knots in the lighter green over the strawberries. Use six strands of thread throughout.

▦ Embroider the cherries, stalks and leaves in satin stitch, using six strands of thread throughout.

▦ When the embroidery is completed, place it face down on a well-padded surface and press lightly, taking care not to crush the stitches.

*Embroider these strawberry and cherry motifs to add a touch of summer to clothes and household linen. They look best worked on a white or pale-colored background to show off the bright red and green of the threads. Use them singly, scattered at random, or in neat rows to make an unusual border pattern.*

*To place the strawberries in the correct position, first tie the ribbon into the desired shape bow. Then mark where the strawberries would look best on the ribbon. Untie the ribbon carefully and mark out the design and embroider it.*

*summer-bright berries*

# CEREMONIAL CHIC

Create a family heirloom by working on the best of materials: a beautiful damask tablecloth, woven with a geometric design. Each square is filled with finely worked circles, triangles and bars in shiny pastels, with zigzags and bars and bows and knots. You could adapt the idea too – wavy lines or circles worked round the damask motifs of any beautiful old linen cloth will be just as original. Or embroider a beautiful length of fabric to make a party skirt or dance frock.

## MATERIALS

*White and silver cotton damask fabric, to make a cloth. (Alternatively, the silver lines can be added to white fabric by machine zigzag lines across the length and width of the* *fabric, using a fine metallic machine thread.)*
*Crewel needle size 6 or 7*
*Crewel needle size 4*
*HB pencil*
*Embroidery hoop*

### Threads
*Susan Bates Anchor stranded cotton in the following colors:*
**blue** *128, 130;* **green** *187, 238, 253;* **kingfisher blue** *433;* **turquoise** *185;* **pale tan** *347;* **yellow** *292, 297;* **pink** *48, 54, 968;* **gray** *397;* **cream** *386;* **beige** *830*
*DMC **fil d'argent** 280*

### Embroidery Stitches
*Satin stitch, straight stitch, cross stitch, knots (see diagram).*

## DIRECTIONS
▦ Use the photographs as a guide to the placement of the motifs and for the colors. Draw the circles, squares and triangles lightly on the fabric with the HB pencil.

▦ Work with the fabric stretched in an embroidery hoop, moving the hoop as each section is completed.

▦ Embroider the circles, squares and triangles in satin stitch using three strands of thread and the finer crewel needle; take care to cover the pencil lines completely.

▦ Work the zigzags and bars at random (without pencil guidelines which would be difficult to conceal) in straight stitch, using either three strands of cotton or one strand of silver thread.

▦ Next, add the cross stitch and the 'V' shapes in straight stitch, again using three strands of cotton or one of silver.

▦ Place the cloth face down on a well-padded surface and press lightly, taking care not to crush the stitches.

▦ Then add the 'bows' by making simple knots, as shown in the diagram, with either six strands of cotton or two strands of silver thread.

▦ To make up the cloth, turn a double hem all round (see page 79 for instructions on mitering corners) and either machine or hand stitch.

*The 'bows' – knotted and cut threads.*

*traditional wedding cloth with a modern gloss*

Multi-sized circles in a haphazard
arrangement are satin-stitched in
a variety of hues.

Mix squares, circles and
triangles, completing the design
with zigzag of color.

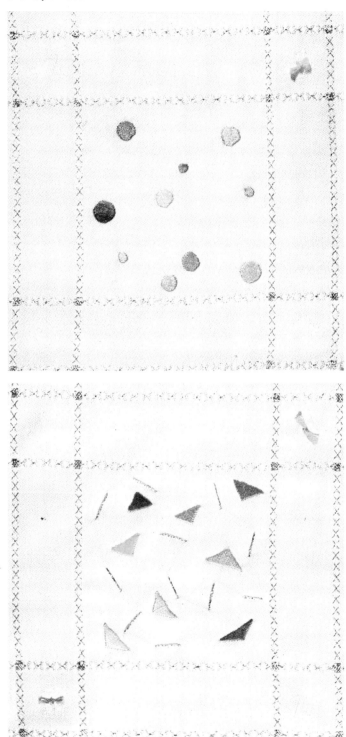

Different colored triangles are
interspersed with bars of silver,
which match the cross stitching.

Small groups of pastel-colored
squares, straight or slanted,
make for a pleasing arrangement.

*Just triangles in bright colors all the same size. Match up with thread bows at the corners.*

*Pick three colors and make up thread bows to fill the square. Add silver cross stitches.*

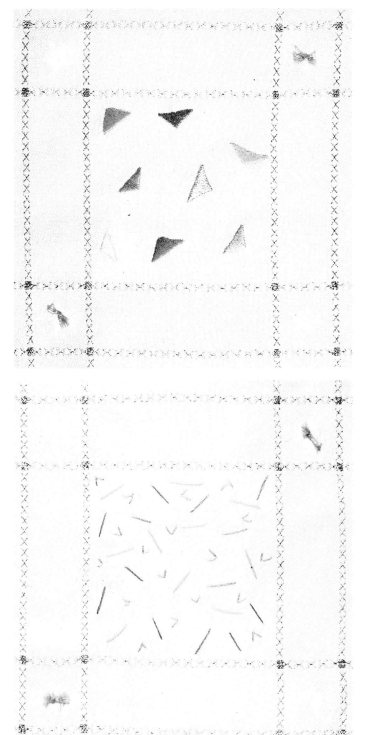

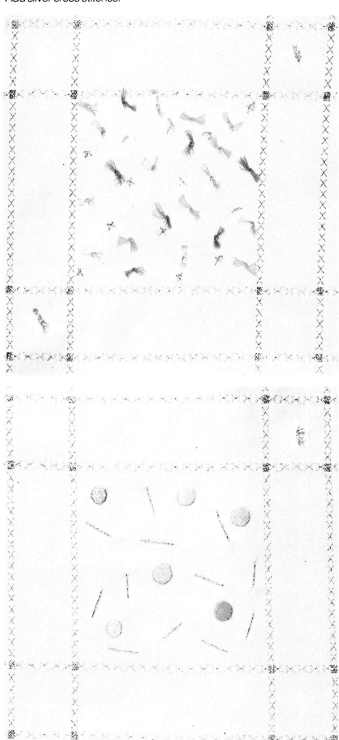

*Stitched bars of yellow and blue mingle with green V-shapes. Complete with thread bows.*

*Similar-sized circles in pastel shades are split up by bars of silver.*

# CYPRUS, PALM AND PINE

Embroidered pictures so often look ornate and out of keeping with modern interiors. But these tree specimens have the delicacy of botanical prints, burnished with a southern sunset. Use a fine, sand-colored linen as a harmonious background, and mount the studies simply between sheets of plastic.

## MATERIALS

| | |
|---|---|
| 22in (55cm) × 22in (55cm) linen or cotton fabric in a neutral color for each tree | Crewel needle size 6 or 7 Large embroidery hoop |

**Threads**
DMC stranded cotton – 1 skein in each of the following colors:
THE PALM TREE: **brown** 433, 938, 3045; **green** 470, 472, 500, 890, 987
THE CYPRESS TREE: **brown** 940, 3032, 3371; **mauve** 413; **green** 500, 502, 503, 504, 924
THE PINE TREE: **green** 500, 580, 732, 937

**Embroidery Stitches**
PALM TREE: satin stitch, straight stitch, long and short stitch.
CYPRESS AND PINE TREES: long and short stitch.

## DIRECTIONS

▦ Enlarge the design to the measurements given on the pattern. Transfer the design to the fabric using one of the methods given on page 6.
▦ Work with the fabric stretched in a large embroidery hoop, moving the hoop as necessary.
▦ Using the diagrams as a color guide, embroider the palm tree in satin stitch and long and short stitch for the trunk, and straight stitch for the fronds. Using the close-up photograph as a guide, embroider the cypress and pine trees in long and short stitch. Use three strands of thread throughout.
▦ When the embroidery is completed, place it face down on a well-padded surface and press lightly, taking care not to crush the stitches.
▦ The pictures can be framed with a conventional frame, or mounted very simply between two sheets of plastic as shown in the photograph.

*Frame the embroidery between two sheets of plastic clipped together. A small strip of double-sided tape can be used on the back of each corner to hold the embroidery in place.*

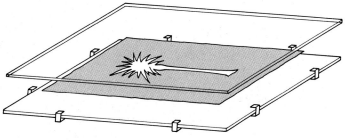

*arboreal portraits*

**Cyprus**
| | |
|---|---|
| **a** | *504* |
| **b** | *503* |
| **c** | *502* |
| **d** | *924* |
| **e** | *413* |
| **f** | *500* |
| **g** | *3371* |
| **h** | *840* |
| **i** | *3032* |

**Palm**
| | |
|---|---|
| **a** | *472* |
| **b** | *987* |
| **c** | *470* |
| **d** | *890* |
| **e** | *500* |
| **f** | *433* |
| **g** | *938* |
| **h** | *3045* |

**Pine**
**a** *732*
**b** *580*
**c** *937*
**d** *500*
**e** *938*
**f** *869*
**g** *780*
**h** *434*

# COUNTRYSIDE DREAMS

Delicate wild roses transform white linen or cotton sheeting into luxurious bedding. One spray looks romantic – several scattered across the fabric cover are a display of consummate skill. The rambling motif looks just as fitting stitched on long curtains of lawn or cotton, which filter the light.

## MATERIALS

| | |
|---|---|
| *White cotton sheet, either single- or double-bed size.* | *Crewel needle size 7 or 8 Embroidery hoop* |

| **Threads** | **Embroidery Stitches** |
|---|---|
| *Susan Bates Anchor stranded cotton in the following colors:* **red** *22, 334;* **pink** *49, 52, 57;* **yellow** *293;* **gold** *306, 307;* **green** *213, 214, 216, 256, 258, 267, 855;* **brown** *905;* **beige** *378;* **cream** *386;* **black** *403;* **white** *1.* | *Stem stitch, padded satin stitch, satin stitch, straight stitch, darning stitch.* |

## DIRECTIONS

▦ Enlarge the design to four times the size of the photograph pattern (see page 6). Transfer the design to the sheet using the pricking and pouncing method given on page 6.

▦ Work with the fabric stretched in an embroidery hoop, moving the hoop as necessary.

▦ Use the photographs as color guides and work with two strands of thread.

▦ Embroider the leaves, stems and rosebuds in closely worked rows of stem stitch to fill each shape.

▦ Embroider the rosehips in padded satin stitch using two shades of red. Work the centers of the roses in satin stitch and pick out the details in straight stitch.

▦ Embroider the rose petals in parallel rows of darning stitch – each stitch should be about ¼in (5mm) long and pick up only one or two threads of fabric.

▦ Work the larger thorns in stem stitch, the smaller ones in straight stitch.

▦ When the embroidery is completed, place it face down on a well-padded surface and press lightly, taking care not to crush the stitches.

*Embroider a section of the spray on a pillowcase to complement the bedcover. Place the motif at the sides of the pillowcase, rather than in the center, to avoid sleeping on the embroidery.*

*wild rose sprays for fine linens*

*Trace off the design and enlarge it (see page 6) so that it is approximately four times larger than the tracing. Transfer it to the sheet using the pricking and pouncing method given on page 6. Use the photograph as a guide to the stitching and the colors. When working the rose petals, keep the stitches of equal size.*

# RAFFIA AND FLOWERS

Richelieu work, traditional European embroidery, surfaces in a novel and simplified form in these embroidered mats. Some of the leaves and flowers use rainbow-colored threads, the shaded colors appearing at random.

## MATERIALS

| | |
|---|---|
| *Circular or oval woven raffia tablemats* | *Chenille needle size 24 Glue and spreader* |

| **Threads** | **Embroidery Stitches** |
|---|---|
| *DMC stranded cotton in the following colors:* **yellow** *307, 973;* **pink** *603, 605, 718;* **red** *321, 606, 815;* **mauve** *553;* **green** *699, 904, 906;* **blue** *792, 703, 704;* **shaded green** *123, 124;* **shaded pink** *116;* **shaded yellow** *104;* **black** *310* | *Buttonhole stitch, long and short stitch, straight stitch.* |

## DIRECTIONS

▦ Trace the designs from the photograph and enlarge them to fit the mats (see page 6). Transfer the design to the mats using the carbon paper method given on page 6.

▦ To prevent the raffia from fraying when the edges are cut, spread a thin film of glue over the narrow areas of the design and the edges of the flowers and leaves, keeping the glue ⅛in (3mm) inside the edges of the design. Leave the mats to dry thoroughly.

▦ Cut away the areas of raffia which are indicated on the design using a sharp pair of scissors.

▦ Use the photograph as a color and stitch guide and work with six strands of thread throughout. Embroider the leaves, joining strips and mat edges in buttonhole stitch and keep the stitches close together to completely cover the raffia beneath.

▦ Edge the flowers in closely worked buttonhole stitch, but with the uprights of the stitches irregularly sized.

▦ Fill in the centers of the flowers with long and short stitch, and pick out the leaf veins with straight stitch.

*Trace the design from this guide, then enlarge it to fit the size of your raffia mats (see page 6).*

# BABY ALPHABET

Straight out of Kate Greenaway, this alphabet layette will be a childhood treasure. The skilled embroiderer can make a quilt for the cot; those less patient could use the appropriate initials to add a little color and individuality to the simplest baby clothes. The letters are formed in padded satin stitch, while the charming figures are easy to copy in long and short stitch. Use pillow cases or quilt covers if you prefer, but remember wadded fabric will not fit into your embroidery hoop.

## MATERIALS

| | |
|---|---|
| 1yd (1m) × 1yd (1m) of white cotton or linen for the cover | pillowcase |
| Ready-made baby cotton or linen | Crewel needle size 6 or 7 |
| | Embroidery hoop |

### Threads
DMC stranded cotton (the colors are given below each diagram and are the ones used for the alphabet in the photograph, but you could substitute other colors if you prefer)
MAIN PART OF LETTERS: **turquoise** 807
FACES, ARMS AND LEGS: **flesh pink** 754
CHEEKS: **pink** 761

### Embroidery Stitches
Padded satin stitch, back stitch, horizontal long and short stitch, straight stitch.

## DIRECTIONS

 Enlarge the design to the desired dimension. Transfer the complete alphabet to the square of white fabric using one of the methods given on page 6 and center it. Transfer two letters to the top corners of the pillowcase, using the photograph as a guide to the placement.

 Using the close-up photographs as a guide to the way stitches are used and the diagrams as color guides, embroider the letters in padded satin stitch with back stitch for the narrow areas. Embroider the figures in horizontal long and short stitch, with straight stitch and back stitch for the outlines, stripes and tiny details. Work with three strands of thread throughout.

 When the embroidery is completed, place it face down on a well-padded surface and press lightly, taking care not to crush the stitches.

 Turn a narrow hem round the cot cover (see page 79 for instructions on mitering corners) and machine or hand stitch.

*Embroider the letters first and then the solid areas of the figures. Lastly, pick out the outlines, stripes and tiny details to give definition.*

*twenty-six ways to say welcome . . .*

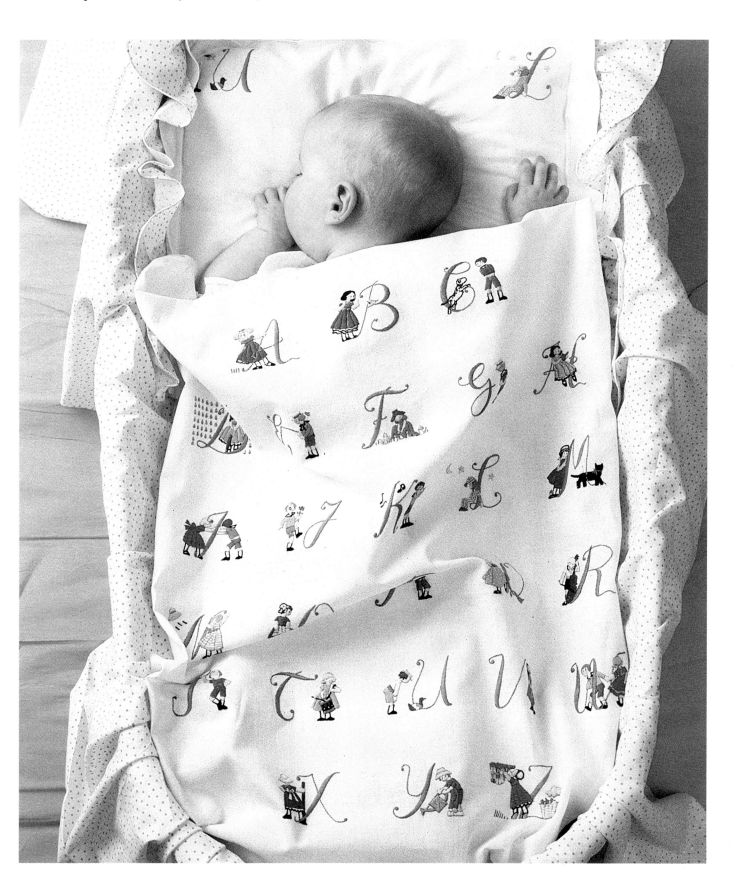

LETTER A: **pink** 957, **yellow** 726, **green** 320, **pink** 3350, **black** 310, **purple** 208

LETTER B: **black** 310, **pink** 3350, **green** 912, **yellow** 726, **blue** 927, **red** 321

LETTER C: **black** 310, **red** 321, **brown** 400, **blue** 826, **purple** 208, **pink** 957

LETTER D: **blue** 927, **brown** 400, **purple** 208, **pink** 957, 3350, **gold** 783, **black** 310

LETTER I: **purple** 208, **turquoise** 806, **yellow** 726, **black** 310, **brown** 400, **pink** 3350, **coral** 351, **green** 954, 320

LETTER J: **tan** 976, **black** 310, **green** 954, **blue** 826, **red** 350

LETTER K: **black** 310, **brown** 400, **tan** 976, **pink** 957, 3350, **blue** 826

LETTER L: **red** 350, **turquoise** 807, **blue** 828, **tan** 976, **yellow** 726

LETTER O: **blue** 826, 828, **brown** 400, **pink** 3350, **flesh pink** 754, **blue** 927, **yellow** 725, **black** 310

LETTER P: **black** 310, **blue** 826, **purple** 208

LETTER Q: **blue** 826, **pink** 957, **gold** 783, **fawn** 613, **black** 310, **white**

LETTER R: **yellow** 726, **green** 954, **brown** 400, **black** 310, **cream** 712

LETTER U: **brown** 400, **coral** 351, **yellow** 725, **cream** 712, **black** 310, **blue** 930, **green** 912, 954

LETTER V: **yellow** 726, **red** 320, **black** 310, **blue** 826, **pink** 3350

LETTER W: **tan** 976, **green** 954, **pink** 957, 3350, **black** 310, **purple** 208

LETTER X: **yellow** 726, **blue** 826, **pink** 3350, **brown** 400, **white**

*LETTER E:* **red** *321, 350,* **blue** *828,* **black** *310,* **tan** *976,* **green** *912,* **gold** *783,* **yellow** *726*

*LETTER F:* **pink** *3350,* **blue** *826,* **tan** *976,* **yellow** *725, 726,* **green** *320,* **fawn** *613,* **cream** *712,* **black** *310*

*LETTER G:* **yellow** *726,* **red** *350,* **gold** *783,* **purple** *208,* **fawn** *613,* **black** *310*

*LETTER H:* **brown** *400,* **red** *350,* **pink** *3350,* **green** *954,* **black** *310,* **white**

### Applying the motifs

*Embroidered letters are an unusual but effective way to personalize clothes and household items, and these letters applied individually will look particularly stylish on baby's toys and clothes. Make sure that Teddy does not wander by marking his T-shirt. A simple bib*

*or baby suit can be given a touch of individuality with the first letter of the owner's name embroidered in a prominent place. And, if you do not have the time to embroider the complete alphabet on a baby quilt, simply embroider baby's name or initials.*

*LETTER M:* **pink** *3350,* **black** *310,* **purple** *208,* **blue** *826*

*LETTER N:* **yellow** *725, 726,* **coral** *351,* **black** *310,* **green** *954,* **gold** *783,* **white**

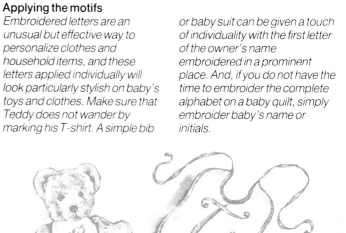

*LETTER S:* **tan** *976,* **purple** *208,* **red** *350,* **black** *310,* **turquoise** *806*

*LETTER T:* **black** *310,* **red** *321,* **green** *954,* **pink** *957,* **yellow** *726,* **blue** *826,* **cream** *712*

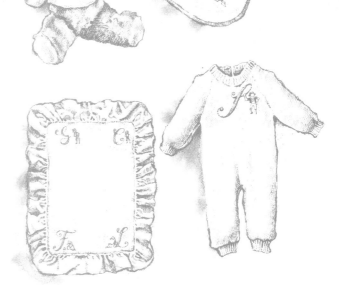

*LETTER Y:* **yellow** *725,* **gold** *783,* **coral** *351,* **blue** *826, 927,* **purple** *208*

*LETTER Z:* **yellow** *725, 726,* **red** *321,* **green** *320, 369,* **turquoise** *806,* **black** *310,* **purple** *208,* **gold** *783,* **brown** *400*

# SEASHELL TRACERY

The delicate traces of seashells are worked in white satin stitch on a padded panel of navy cotton chintz. The embroidered square is then bordered with navy-and-white-striped cotton and navy chintz – the entire panel is attached to a plain white cotton sheet to create a stylish bed throw.

## MATERIALS

| | |
|---|---|
| 1½yd (1.5m) × 45in (115cm) wide navy blue cotton chintz | White dress marking chalk |
| 2ft (60cm) × 2ft (60cm) polyester wadding | Knitting needle |
| | White sewing thread |
| 2ft (60cm) × 2ft (60cm) fine calico | Chenille needle size 18 or 20 |
| 28in (70cm) × 36in (90cm) wide navy-and-white-striped cotton | Navy sewing thread |
| | White cotton sheet, single-bed size |

| **Thread** | **Embroidery Stitch** |
|---|---|
| 2oz (50gm) ball of white knitting cotton, sport weight | Satin stitch |

## DIRECTIONS

▦ From the navy chintz cut out one square 24in (62cm) × 24½in (62cm) and four strips each 7½in (19cm) × 41in (103cm).

▦ From the striped cotton cut four strips 2¼in (5.5cm) × 25½in (64cm) wide, across the stripes.

▦ Enlarge the design to the dimensions given on the pattern.

▦ Pierce each small dot on the full-size pattern with the point of the knitting needle, then place the pattern over the chintz square and mark the dots on the right side of the fabric with the dress marking chalk.

▦ Place wadding between the chintz and the calico, making sure the chintz is right side up. There should be ⅜in (1cm) surplus of chintz all round the square. Pin through the three layers to hold them in place before tacking together vertically and horizontally, using the white sewing thread.

▦ Embroider the dots in satin stitch with the knitting cotton. Then work the remaining motifs in the same way, using the diagram as a guide to the placement.

▦ Remove the tacking threads and press the ⅜in (1cm) surplus of chintz to the wrong side, taking care not to flatten the wadding.

▦ To make the narrow striped border, machine stitch the striped sections together at the corners as shown in the diagram using the navy thread.

▦ To make the wide chintz 'frame' machine stitch the chintz strips at the four angles shown in the diagram.

▦ Place the striped border

# navy and white simplicity

centered on the white sheet and pin it in position. Then put the embroidered chintz square in the center of the striped border and tack in position. Machine stitch around the edge of the square, keeping the stitches as close to the edge as possible. Remove the tacking thread.

▦ Turn and press a ⅜in (1cm) hem on the inner and outer edges of the chintz 'frame' and position it around the edge of the striped border, overlapping it by ⅜in (1cm) to hide the raw edges. Pin and then tack it in place. Machine stitch around the inner and outer edges of the 'frame', as close to the edge as possible. Remove the tacking stitches.

▦ Press the chintz frame and border carefully, but do not press the embroidered chintz square or the wadding will be flattened.

*Taking inspiration from nature, the stylized forms of the shells above have been reproduced on the bed throw. By simplifying other natural forms, an endless variety of fascinating designs can be created.*

*The shell shapes are worked in dots and blocks of satin stitch on the central padded section. This is framed firstly by a narrow striped border and then by a wide, plain navy blue border.*

# A POCKETFUL OF FLOWERS

Choose any well-made blouse or shirt and work a little magic to make a flower spray blossom from the pocket. Honeysuckle, bluebells and violets all trail prettily and are simple to embroider.

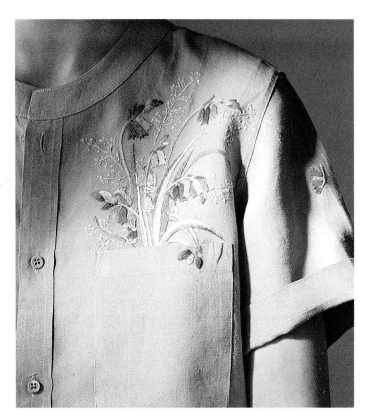

## MATERIALS

Ready-made shirt with a plain patch pocket on the chest 10in (25cm) × 10in (25cm) muslin or fine cotton (if shirt fabric is fine or delicate)
Crewel needles sizes 4, 6 and 8
Embroidery hoop

### Thread
DMC stranded embroidery cotton in the following shades:
FOR THE BLUEBELLS 1 skein of each:
**blue** 322, 798, 800, 813; **green** 368, 369, 502, 504, 966, 989; **pink** 224, 842; **yellow** 734
FOR THE HONEYSUCKLE 1 skein of each:
**green** 368, 704, 988, 989; **yellow** 725, 781, 783, 3078; **pink** 225, 316, 356, 739, 758, 760
FOR THE VIOLETS 1 skein of each:
**green** 368, 937, 966, 988, 989; **mauve** and **pink** 224, 225, 315, 316, 778; **yellow** 726

### Embroidery Stitches
BLUEBELLS: long and short stitch, satin stitch, stem stitch, straight stitch.
HONEYSUCKLE: long and short stitch, satin stitch, stem stitch, Chinese knots.
VIOLETS: long and short stitch, satin stitch and stem stitch.

## DIRECTIONS

▦ Transfer the design to the front of the shirt by either the carbon paper or transfer pencil method given on page 6 and positioning it as shown in the photographs. Transfer a single flower to the top of the adjacent sleeve.

▦ If the fabric to be embroidered is fine or delicate, work with both the shirt and the muslin (or cotton) stretched in an embroidery hoop. Cut away the central portion of the muslin to expose the area to be worked. Repeat with a second square of muslin if the design will not fit completely into the hoop, and the hoop needs to be moved.

▦ When working the embroidery use the photographs and diagrams as color guides.

▦ FOR THE BLUEBELLS, embroider the flowers and leaves in long and short stitch, using satin stitch for the narrow areas. Work the stems of the bluebells and the background foliage in stem stitch, adding groups of straight stitches in pink. Use two strands of thread throughout.

▦ FOR THE HONEYSUCKLE, embroider the flowers and leaves in long and short stitch, using satin stitch for the narrow areas. Work the stems and stamens in stem stitch, and the pistils and pollen in Chinese knots. Use two strands of thread for the flowers, leaves and stems; one strand for the stamens; three strands for the pollen, and six strands for the pistils.

▦ FOR THE VIOLETS, embroider the flowers and leaves in long and short stitch, using satin stitch for the flower centers. Work the stems and leaf veins in stem stitch. Use two strands of thread throughout.

▦ When the embroidery is completed place the shirt face down on a well-padded surface and press lightly, taking care not to crush the stitches.

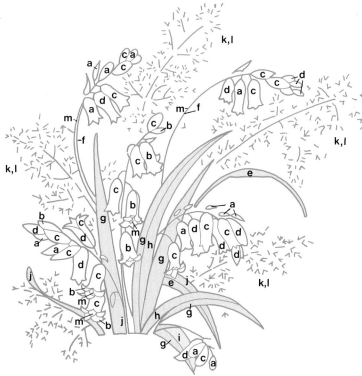

**Bluebell**
**a** 798, **b** 800, **c** 813, **d** 322, **e** 989, **f** 966, **g** 502, **h** 504, **i** 368, **j** 369, **k** 842, **l** 224, **m** 734

# *floral detail for a classic blouse*

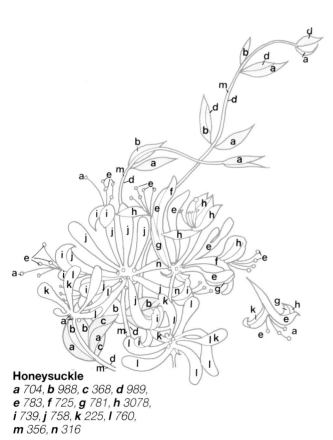

**Honeysuckle**
*a* 704, *b* 988, *c* 368, *d* 989,
*e* 783, *f* 725, *g* 781, *h* 3078,
*i* 739, *j* 758, *k* 225, *l* 760,
*m* 356, *n* 316

**Violet**                    *e* 989, *f* 224, *g* 315, *h* 316,
*a* 368, *b* 966, *c* 937, *d* 988,     *i* 778, *j* 225, *k* 726

# MEDITERRANEAN GARLAND

That occasional chair which fills an unused corner can become an appealing conversation piece with just a little thought. A garland of mimosa, poppies, wild roses, carnations, fuchsias, orange blossom and oleander, with its attendant butterfly and ladybirds, twines around the edge of a drop-in chair seat. To give the appearance of an all-over tapestry cover – with none of the hard work – a patterned damask brocade is used, its geometric pattern cleverly offsetting the summer blooms.

## MATERIALS

Piece of upholstery-weight fabric. To calculate the amount measure the width of your chair, from side to side and from back to front, and add 2in (5cm) to each measurement. Crewel needle size 5 or 6. Embroidery hoop.

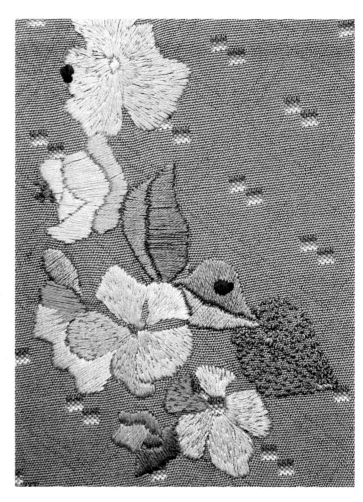

### Threads
DMC stranded cotton – 1 skein of each of the following colors: **ecru** and **white**; **pink** 223, 224, 225, 316, 605, 778, 818, 819, 3688, 3689; **green** 320, 367, 471, 502, 503, 504, 912, 3053, 3347, 3348; **red** 325, 350; **coral** 351; **turquoise** 578; **gold** 676; **yellow** 725, 727, 742, 743, 744, 745, 3078; **bronze** 734; **peach** 754, 945, 951; **beige** 739; **blue** 828, 3325; **blue/gray** 927, 928

### Embroidery Stitches
Satin stitch, long and short stitch, seed stitch, stem stitch, padded satin stitch.

## DIRECTIONS

▦ Enlarge the design to fit the chair seat (see page 6). Transfer the design to the fabric using the carbon paper method given on page 6, positioning the garland centrally on the fabric.

▦ Work with the fabric in an embroidery hoop, moving the hoop as necessary. Using the photograph and diagram as guides, embroider the flowers and leaves in satin stitch and long and short stitch, and pick out the details at the center of the flowers with seed stitch. Work the stems in stem stitch, and the flower buds and the spray of mimosa in padded satin stitch. Use three strands of thread throughout.

▦ When the embroidery is completed, place it face down on a well-padded surface and press lightly, taking care not to crush the stitches.

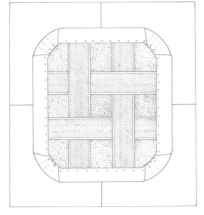 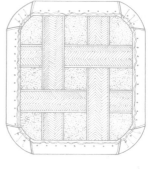 

▦ Knock out the seat from the chair. Remove the hessian base and the old top cover from the seat using a ripping chisel and hammer.

▦ Mark center of embroidery on all sides. Place the embroidery wrong side up on a flat surface. Center the chair seat over the embroidery, making sure that the design is facing in the right direction.

▦ Pull the embroidered fabric firmly to the underside of the seat and tack in place, working from the center of each side outwards. Tack each corner in position, smoothing over the fabric to give a rounded effect.

▦ Cut a piece of hessian on the straight of grain the size of the chair seat base. Turn under the raw edges and tack in place all round the seat covering the edges of the embroidered fabric and rounding the corners.

*a reminder of warm, fragrant days*

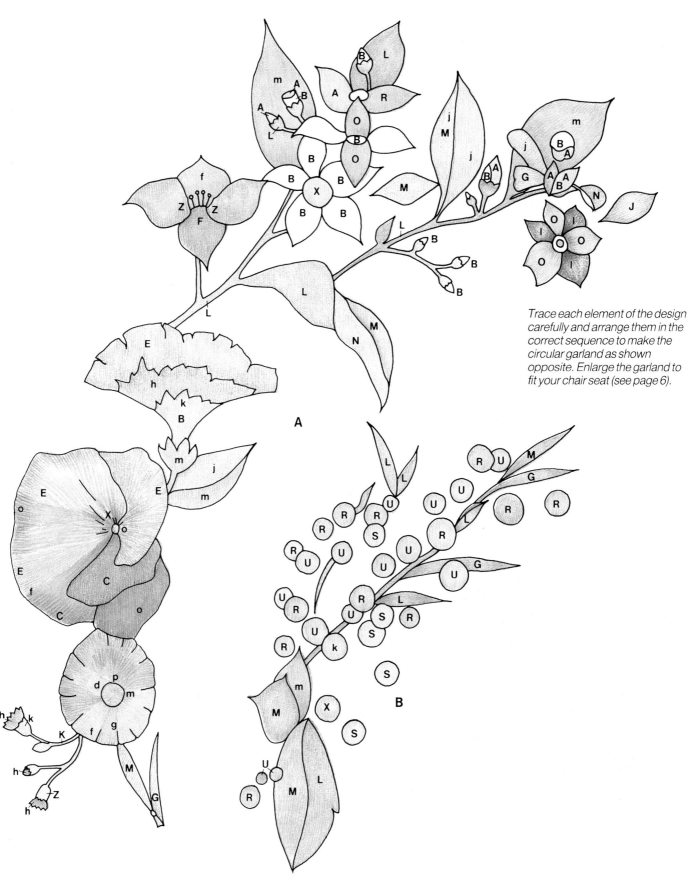

*Trace each element of the design carefully and arrange them in the correct sequence to make the circular garland as shown opposite. Enlarge the garland to fit your chair seat (see page 6).*

**KEY**

| | |
|---|---|
| A | ecru |
| B | white |
| C | 223 |
| D | 224 |
| E | 225 |
| F | 316 |
| G | 320 |
| H | 350 |
| I | 351 |
| J | 367 |
| K | 471 |
| L | 502 |
| M | 503 |
| N | 504 |
| O | 598 |
| P | 605 |
| Q | 676 |
| R | 725 |
| S | 727 |
| T | 734 |
| U | 742 |
| V | 743 |
| W | 744 |
| X | 745 |
| Y | 754 |
| Z | 778 |
| a | 739 |
| b | 818 |
| c | 819 |
| d | 828 |
| e | 912 |
| f | 927 |
| g | 928 |
| h | 945 |
| i | 951 |
| j | 3055 |
| k | 3078 |
| l | 3325 |
| m | 3347 |
| n | 3348 |
| o | 3688 |
| p | 3689 |
| q | 326 |

# FISH FANTASY

A fine collection of fish with their asymmetrical shapes and gorgeous details has been caught and laid out for display – embroider them in hot, tropical colors for cushions as stunning as pictures. Don't labor over the close regularity of the stitches; on a white background the gaps will give you a painterly quality.

## MATERIALS

| | |
|---|---|
| 25in (63cm) × 18in (48cm) white cotton fabric | Crewel needle size 6 or 7 Embroidery hoop |

### Threads
*DMC stranded cotton – 1 skein of each of the following:*
CUSHION A: **blue** *517, 518, 519, 747;* **yellow** *704;* **pink** *956;* **pale green** *955;* **shaded green** *123*
CUSHION B: **green** *699, 702, 704;* **shaded green** *114;* **orange** *970, 972;* **yellow** *973;* **black** *310*
CUSHION C: **green** *699, 701, 890;* **blue** *797, 809;* **kingfisher** *996;* **shaded blue** *113;* **yellow** *973;* **red** *606;* **black** *310*

### Embroidery Stitches
*Long and short stitch, satin stitch, straight stitch.*

## DIRECTIONS

⊞ Enlarge the design to the measurements given on the pattern (see page 6). Transfer the design to the fabric using one of the methods given on page 6 and positioning it as shown in the diagram.
⊞ Work with the fabric stretched in an embroidery hoop, moving the hoop as necessary.
⊞ Using the close-up photograph as a stitch guide, embroider the fish in long and short stitch and in satin stitch, and pick out the details in straight stitch. Use three strands of thread throughout.
⊞ When the embroidery is completed, place it face down on a well-padded surface and press lightly, taking care not to crush the stitches.
⊞ Instructions for making up the cushion covers are on page 79.

56

# streamlined shapes, bright bodies

Trace the fish designs from these pictures, which are also guides to the colors used on each fish. The photograph above shows how the embroidery is worked to allow the fabric to show through.

# OAK LEAVES AND ACORNS

The couturier Schiaperelli loved creating surreal button designs and these oak leaves and acorns remind one of her inventiveness. Real acorns, threaded through with cord, make unusual buttons, and the acorn motifs embroidered around the buttonholes, on the cuffs, and on the lapels of the dark woolen blazer complement them perfectly.

*Sleeve decoration.*

*Remove the cups from eight acorns and make a hole through each cup. Thread the cord through the hole and make a knot inside the cup. Glue the cup securely on to the acorn before varnishing.*

*Buttonhole and button.*

## MATERIALS

| | |
|---|---|
| *Ready-made woolen jacket with a fairly smooth weave* | *Card* |
| *16 acorns with cups* | *Polyurethane varnish* |
| *8 short lengths of thin cord in matching or contrasting colors to the embroidery threads* | *Small paintbrush* |
| | *Glue* |
| | *White dress marking chalk* |
| | *Crewel needle size 3 or 4* |
| | *Large chenille needle* |

| **Threads** | **Embroidery Stitch** |
|---|---|
| *DMC stranded cotton:* | *Satin stitch.* |
| **pale green** *368;* **dull gold** *834* | |

## DIRECTIONS

▦ To prepare the acorn 'buttons' thread short lengths of cord through eight acorns, as shown in the diagrams. Remove the cups from the remaining acorns and make a hole through each one as shown. Using a small paintbrush, seal the acorns with the varnish and hang them up to dry; allow twenty-four hours for the varnish to dry thoroughly.

▦ Trace the leaf shapes and transfer them to card. Make a set of templates by carefully cutting round each leaf with a sharp pair of scissors. Using the photographs as a guide, position the templates on the jacket – on the lapels, the edge of the sleeves and round each of the buttonholes – and draw round them with a dress marking chalk.

▦ Embroider the leaves in satin stitch using six strands of thread, taking care to cover the guide lines.

▦ Attach the acorn 'buttons' opposite the buttonholes.

▦ Thread each cord of the other set of acorns through the large chenille needle, pull the cords through to the reverse of the jacket and knot each one securely.

*autumnal harvest for winter days*

# FRUIT NEEDLEPOINT

The soft colors of this needlepoint fruit basket suggest the aging tones of gentle Dutch seventeenth-century still lifes. The embroidery is worked in half cross stitch on linen – the natural color of the fabric provides the perfect neutral background for the fine needlework.

## MATERIALS

24cm (60cm) × 32in (80cm) light brown even-weave 24-gauge linen

Crewel needle size 5 or 6
Embroidery hoop

### Threads
Danish flower threads –
1 skein of each of the following colors: **green** 40, 222, 223, 302; **red** 53, 93; **violet** 5, 230; **yellow** 28, 225; **fawn** 7
DMC stranded cotton –
3 skeins of **green** 989
2 skeins of each of the following colors:
**green** 472, 3346, 3348; **coral** 353; **peach** 754; **beige** 644
1 skein of each of the following colors:
**green** 368, 471, 581, 3051, 3052, 3053, 3347; **bronze** 733, 734; **rust** 355, 356; **tan** 922; **coral** 352; **peach** 758, 945, 950, 951; **pink** 316, 760, 778, 948; **mauve** 3041, 3042; **yellow** 745, 3078; **cream** 746; **gold** 437, 677, 833, 834, 3046; **fawn** 422, 738; **brown** 420, 640, 642; **beige** 437, 712, 739; **gray** 452, 453, 646, 647, 3023

### Embroidery Stitch
Half cross stitch: each square on the chart represents one half cross stitch worked over two vertical and two horizontal fabric threads.

## DIRECTIONS

 Run a vertical and a horizontal line of basting through the center of the linen to correspond with the center lines on the chart.

 Work with the fabric stretched in an embroidery hoop, moving the hoop as necessary.

 Embroider the design outwards from the center in half cross stitch, following the picture on page 63 and using the colors and threads indicated: the main part of the picture is worked using five strands of the stranded cotton, while some areas are stitched with a combination of Danish flower thread and stranded cotton threaded through the needle together.

 When the embroidery is completed, place it face down on a well-padded surface and press lightly, taking care not to crush the stitches.

 If the fabric has become distorted during the stitching, it will need to be blocked (see page 79). The embroidery should be framed professionally.

*mellow colors, mellow fruits*

**A.   Vine leaves, tendrils and stalks**
*green* 40, 47, 223, 368, 471, 472, 581, 989, 3051, 3052, 3053, 3446, 3347, 3348
*brown* 420, 640
*gray* 646, 647
*fawn* 422

**B.   Basket**
*gray* 646, 3023
*rust* 356
*beige* 644
*fawn* 7
*green* 222, 302, 3052

**C.   Cherries**
*pink* 948
*peach* 754, 758
*rust* 355, 356
*coral* 352
*tan* 922
*red* 53, 93
*green* 368

**D. Green grapes**
*bronze* 734
*green* 472
*cream* 746
*fawn* 422, 738
*gold* 833, 834, 3046, 3047
*yellow* 225, 3078

**E.   Black grapes**
*mauve* 3041, 3042
*violet* 5, 230
*pink* 316, 778
*green* 581

**F.   Apple**
*pink* 760, 948
*peach* 754, 950
*green* 472
*coral* 353
*beige* 350, 712
*yellow* 745, 3078

**G.   Left pear**
*peach* 945, 950, 951
*beige* 437, 739
*gold* 677
*green* 223, 368, 3348
*yellow* 28
*pink* 948
*fawn* 422

**H.   Right pear**
*peach* 945, 950
*beige* 437, 712
*gold* 677
*green* 472
*yellow* 3078
*fawn* 422
*brown* 642
*gray* 452, 647

**I.   Peach at the back**
*peach* 754
*pink* 760, 948
*coral* 353
*yellow* 745
*beige* 712
*fawn* 738
*gray* 452, 453

**J.   Front peach**
*peach* 754, 950
*pink* 760
*coral* 352, 353
*yellow* 745, 3078
*beige* 712
*gray* 452, 453, 647

**K.   Fruit inside basket**
*green* 472, 989, 3051, 3346, 3347
*rust* 355

*The diagram indicates the different fruits and can be used with this list of colors.*

# COUNTRYSIDE MOSAIC

Each of the nine canvas squares that make up this tapestry mosaic contain a different wildlife scene, but they cleverly combine to create a complete picture – poppies and ladybirds, frogs on lily pads, butterflies and milkweed, snails and dandelions are just some of them. If you feel that the complete mosaic is beyond you, make up just a couple of the individual scenes.

## MATERIALS

9 squares of single thread 12-gauge canvas, each 14½in (36cm) × 14½in (36cm)
Tapestry needle size 18 or 20
3ft (90cm) × 3ft (90cm) beige

cotton fabric
Matching sewing thread
Fine-tip waterproof felt marker
Embroidery frame

### Threads
DMC tapestry wool in the colors given beside each panel.

### Embroidery Stitches
Tent stitch, Chinese knots, straight stitch, herringbone stitch, back stitch.

Each square of the design is complete in itself, but can be combined with others to make a larger scene. When all the squares are embroidered and blocked, arrange them as shown in the diagrams opposite. Join the squares with flat seams using backstitch (see page 7), and press open.

For a larger bedspread, slipstitch the completed embroidery on to a plain bedspread. Move the panel around the bedspread until the desired effect is achieved. For a wall hanging, make a casing at the top and bottom edge and insert two bamboo canes and hang with a cord.

## DIRECTIONS

▦ Draw a vertical line with the marker through the center of each canvas square, taking care not to cross any vertical threads. Mark the central horizontal line in the same way. Then rule corresponding lines across the chart to find the center of the design.

▦ Work each of the individual canvas squares in an embroidery frame.

▦ Work the designs outwards from the center in tent stitch and pick out the details in Chinese knots and straight stitch as indicated on the charts.

▦ When all the squares have been embroidered, block each one carefully (see page 79), making sure that they are all the same size: each blocked square should measure approximately 10in (25cm) × 10in (25cm).

▦ Following the diagram, join the squares into three strips of three squares, by making a back-stitched seam between each square. Press each seam open.

▦ Join the strips together in the same way, and again press each seam open.

▦ On the reverse of the cover, turn in the surplus canvas round the edge (see page 79 for instructions on mitering corners) and secure it with a row of herringbone stitch.

▦ To make the lining, cut a 33in (82cm) square from the beige fabric. Turn and press a hem round the edge to make a 31in (78cm) square. Slipstitch the lining to the bedcover and press it gently, taking care not to crush the stitches.

1

**1. Dandelions and snail**
*green* 7320, 7347, 7370, 7548; *brown* 7419, 7468, 7526; *turquoise* 7302; *orange* 7767; *beige* 7465; *cream* 7141; *blue* 7800; *gray* 7331, 7620; *yellow* 7473, 7727, 7742, 7905; *white*

**2. Bee with flowers**
*cream* 7503; *pink* 7135, 7136, 7640; *gray* 7618, 7624; *blue* 7799; *green* 7339, 7363, 7396, 7398; *turquoise* 7592; *brown* 7417, 7419, 7479, 7485, 7713, 7999; *black*; *white*

**3. Ladybird and poppies**
*green* 7347, 7427, 7770; *tan* 7947; *red* 7107, 7606; *blue* 7799; *brown* 7401, 7415, 7419, 7801; *gray* 7618, 7713; *yellow*

7078, 7485; **white**; **black**; **ecru**

**4. Dragonfly and flowers**
**yellow** 7484, 7504, 7579, 7678, 7843; **brown** 7417, 7469, 7479,

7526; **green** 7353, 7362, 7363, 7389, 7404, 7408, 7427, 7429; **blue** 7243, 7791; **turquoise** 7302, 7326, 7329, 7592, 7690; **mauve** 7245; **cream** 7493;

kingfisher 7650; **black**; **white**

**5. Grasshopper and berries**
**brown** 7513, 7526, 7548, 7713, 7833, 7999; **green** 7346, 7353,

7362, 7363, 7376, 7384, 7392, 7396, 7493, 7861; **yellow** 7473, 7485, 7785; **beige** 7450; **red** 7606, 7666, 7946; **turquoise** 7302, 7592; **black**; **white**

**6. Frog and waterlily**
**brown** 7249, 7355, 7490, 7801;
**green** 7362, 7636, 7384, 7540;
**yellow** 7485, 7677, 7678; **pink**
7356, 7543, 7950; **black**; **white**

**7. Newt and flowers**
**green** 7320, 7362, 7363, 7384,
7389, 7393, 7398, 7890; **brown**
7249, 7512, 7526, 7999; **yellow**
7678, 7782, 7784, 7785; **cream**
7501; **beige** 7450; **turquoise**
7592; **black**; **white**

**8. Butterflies and flowers**
**brown** 7514, 7538, 7713, 7780;

**green** 7320, 7363, 7384, 7387,
7583, 7890; **yellow** 7504, 7678,
7786; **pink** 7255; **mauve** 7245;
**turquoise** 7996; **orange** 7505,
7946; **red** 7666; **blue** 7317,
7796; **tan** 7457; **black**; **white**;
**ecru**

**9. Beetles and flowers**
**yellow** 7677, 7784, 7786; **green**
7320, 7367, 7386, 7389, 7424,
7548, 7583, 7890, 7956; **brown**
7479, 7526, 7713, 7845, 7846;
**beige** 7450, 7463; **mauve** 7245;
**pink** 7255; **blue** 7317, 7820,
7995; **white**; **ecru**

# PANSY BAG

Pansies – *pensées* means thoughts – are just the motif for a useful carry-all for books, holiday things, or weekend bits and pieces. The bag is stitched in sturdy cotton first and the embroidered canvas panel is attached afterwards.

## MATERIALS

32in (80cm) × 45in (115cm) heavy gray cotton fabric
7½in (19cm) × 18½in (46cm) gray lining fabric
20in (50cm) × 22in (55cm) double-thread 10-gauge canvas

6½in (16cm) × 17in (43cm) stout card
Gray sewing thread
Fine-tip waterproof pen
Fabric glue
Tapestry needle size 18 or 20
Embroidery frame

### Threads

*Susan Bates Anchor tapestry wool*
TARTAN BACKGROUND
4 skeins of **gray** 400; 3 skeins of **beige** 438; 5 skeins of **blue** 147; 5 skeins of **green** 164; 2 skeins of **green** 506.
THE PANSIES
1 skein of each color:
**green** 213, 215, 243, 265, 861; **yellow** 264, 288, 290, 297, 305, 306, 729; **beige** 377, 390, 711, 732; **white** 402; **pink** 337, 421, 570, 661, 732, 835, 892; **blue** 850, 851

### Embroidery Stitch

*Half cross stitch: each square on the chart represents one half cross stitch.*

## DIRECTIONS

THE PANSY EMBROIDERY:

▦ Draw a 17in (43cm) × 14½in (36cm) rectangle centered on the canvas with the felt marker. Then draw a vertical and a horizontal line in the center of this rectangle, taking care not to cross any threads running the opposite way. Rule corresponding lines across the printed chart to find the center.

▦ Work with the canvas in a frame. Begin stitching at the center of the canvas, working outwards and following the chart square by square. Embroider the pansy design first and then fill in the background with the tartan pattern.

▦ Block the finished piece of embroidery (see page 79).

▦ Trim the surplus canvas away leaving a margin of 1in (2.5cm) all round the embroidery. Turn in the margin (see page 79 for instructions on mitering corners) and tack round the edge.

TO MAKE THE BAG:

▦ Cut out the fabric as shown in the cutting layout. Join the front and back pieces together along the shortest sides using a fell seam with a seam allowance of ⅝in (1.5cm). Turn over ⅜in (1cm) followed by 1in (2.5cm) along the top of the bag, right-side up, to make a double hem; topstitch ¼in (5mm) away from the edge.

▦ Fold each strap piece in half lengthwise with the right side of the fabric on the inside. Stitch ⅜in (1cm) from the edge. Turn the straps to the right side and press flat. Top stitch all the way round ¼in (5mm) from the edge.

▦ Pin one strap to the front of the bag and one to the back along the lines indicated on the pattern and stitch in place securely.

▦ Turn the bag inside out and pin the base piece in place (with a seam allowance of ⅝in (1.5cm)). Stitch round the base twice. Turn the bag right side out and slipstitch the embroidered panel to the front.

▦ Cover the card with the lining fabric, as shown in the diagram, and let the glue dry thoroughly, then drop the base into the bag and push well down.

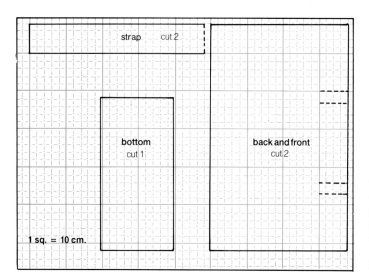

*Assemble the bag by joining the front and back sections. Make the straps and attach them securely before sewing the base in position. Slipstitch the canvas work panel to the front of the bag before inserting the stiffened base panel*

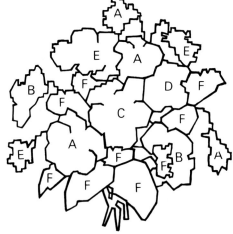

| Tartan pattern | | 10 | 265 | 7 | 337 | 3 | 661 |
|---|---|---|---|---|---|---|---|
| 1 | 400 | 11 | 288 | 8 | 570 | 4 | 402 |
| 2 | 506 | | | 9 | 243 | 5 | 732 |
| 3 | 438 | | | | | 6 | 421 |
| 4 | 147 | **Flowers B** | | **Flowers D** | | 7 | 892 |
| | | 1 | 661 | 1 | 850 | 8 | 570 |
| **Flowers A** | | 2 | 570 | 2 | 306 | 9 | 711 |
| 1 | 850 | 3 | 421 | 3 | 305 | 10 | 297 |
| 2 | 264 | 4 | 305 | 4 | 297 | 11 | 243 |
| 3 | 306 | | | 5 | 402 | | |
| 4 | 711 | **Flowers C** | | 6 | 732 | **Leaves F** | |
| 5 | 390 | 1 | 851 | 7 | 570 | 1 | 213 |
| 6 | 243 | 2 | 290 | | | 2 | 215 |
| 7 | 297 | 3 | 402 | **Flowers E** | | 3 | 861 |
| 8 | 402 | 4 | 390 | 1 | 850 | 4 | 438 |
| 9 | 305 | 5 | 835 | 2 | 306 | 5 | 377 |
| | | 6 | 729 | | | | |

# MAJOLICA MAT

A familiar image of the Mediterranean, blue and white tiles with their formal, often ornate, designs inspired this idea for a floor mat. Each square is worked separately mainly in cross stitch, then enriched with back stitch and Chinese knots to give the geometric precision of tiles. You have a wealth of designs here to make up as shown, or to adapt for your own ideas – table mats, cushions, chairbacks, folder covers, or a series of framed patterns. If you are ambitious, the mat itself could be enlarged by repeating a combination of the squares.

## MATERIALS

20 squares of Pingouin rug canvas, each 20in (50cm) × 20in (50cm)

Large tapestry or rug needle

### Threads
Pingouin rug wool: 40 hanks of **white** 05; 15 hanks of **blue** 67; 9 hanks of **blue** 31; 8 hanks of **blue** 65; 7 hanks of **blue** 40; 2 hanks of each of the following colors: **blue** 13, 32, 66, 134; 1 hank of **blue** 28

### Embroidery Stitches
Cross stitch, back stitch, Chinese knots, herringbone stitch and half cross stitch.

## DIRECTIONS

THE CHARTS:

▦ Use chart A for the four corner squares; charts B and C for the ten border squares that make up the garland, and charts 1, 2, 3 and 4 to make up the six central geometric squares: D, E, F, G.

▦ Embroider each square from the appropriate chart. Work squares A, B and C in cross stitch. Work the geometric squares in cross stitch and pick out extra details in back stitch and Chinese knots. Then embroider two rows of back stitch vertically and horizontally across the center of each square using colour 40.

▦ When all the squares have been embroidered, block each one carefully (see page 79), making sure that they are all the same size: each blocked square should measure 17in (40cm) × 16in (40cm).

▦ Following the arrangement in the diagram, join the squares into four strips of five squares with

back stitched seams. Press the seams open.

▦ Join the strips together in the same way, making sure that the pattern is correct.

▦ On the reverse side of the rug, turn in the surplus canvas and secure it with herringbone stitch. Secure the surplus canvas along each seam in a similar way, using herring bone stitch.

▦ On the top side of the rug, use color 40 to conceal the seams – work rows of back stitch along them – and to finish the edges off work a row of half cross stitch round the outside of the rug.

*Once you have mastered this rug, try using different 'tiles'.*

72

# ceramic art in blue and white

This rug is made up of twenty sections of canvas work each measuring 16in (40cm) square. Embroider each of the sections systematically from the charts, beginning with the four corner squares which are worked from chart A. Charts B and C are followed to work the ten sections which complete the garland border. The border sections are worked in cross stitch.

The central portion of the rug is made up of six geometrically patterned sections worked in cross stitch, back stitch and Chinese knots. These sections are worked from charts 1, 2, 3 and 4 using different combinations of the pattern charts as shown in the plan.

There are various methods of making a rug non-slip. The simplest way is to coat the turned-under edges of the canvas with rubber-based adhesive and leave them to dry thoroughly.

A heavy lining also works well. Cut a piece of hessian slightly larger than the finished rug and turn under the raw edges. Slipstitch the hessian to the wrong side of the rug, as shown in the diagram.

Alternatively, non-slip netting can be purchased. This is cut slightly smaller than the rug and placed between it and the floor.

One section of the rug design can be worked and made into a cushion cover. Finish the edges in the same way as for the pansy bag (see page 70), and slipstitch it to a ready-made cushion cover.

This diagram shows the final arrangement of squares. The outer border is made up of fourteen squares (patterns A, B and C) and the six inner squares are composites, using the four small patterns opposite.

# PRECIOUS PURSES

Little purses with the charm of the antique – they are not meant to be practical but to be appreciated, toyed with like a piece of grandma's jewelry. They are stitched in old-fashioned petit point, using soft-colored threads. They do take a little time to make, but then time is precious and gives them value.

## MATERIALS FOR SMALL PURSE

2 pieces of double-thread 18-gauge canvas, each 7in (17cm) × 5in (13cm)
2 pieces of dark green lining

fabric, each 4¼in (11cm) × 3in (8cm)
Matching sewing thread
Tapestry needle size 24

### Threads
Susan Bates Anchor stranded cotton
2 skeins of **dark green** 212
1 skein of each of the following colors: **pink** 72, 75, 77; **green** 230, 240, 257; **mauve** 105; **red** 19, 46, 334

### Embroidery Stitches
Tent stitch, back stitch, herringbone stitch.

## DIRECTIONS

Working the front and back pieces:

▣ Run a vertical and a horizontal line of guide basting through the centers of each piece of canvas, taking care not to cross any threads running the opposite way. Match these to the corresponding lines on the chart to find the center of the design.

▣ Working from the center outwards, embroider the design from the chart in tent stitch, following the picture carefully.

▣ When the embroidery is completed, block it (see page 79), making sure that the front and back pieces are exactly the same size.

▣ To make up the purse, trim away the surplus canvas round each piece of embroidery, leaving a margin of ⅜in (1cm).

▣ Using back stitch, join the front and back pieces.

▣ Turn over the ⅜in (1cm) margin at the top of the bag and secure it neatly with a row of herringbone stitch.

▣ Cut out the lining ⅜in (1cm) larger than the completed embroidery and join the seam. Turn and press a ⅜in (1cm) hem round the top of the lining and slipstitch it to the top of the bag,

leaving a ¾in (2cm) gap at one side over the seam.

▣ Make a twisted cord approximately 6in (16cm) long from 8 lengths of stranded cotton in dark green and decorate it with a tassel as shown in the photograph.

▣ Slipstitch the cord to the top of the bag, tucking the two ends into the gap in the lining. Stitch across the gap to secure the ends of the cord.

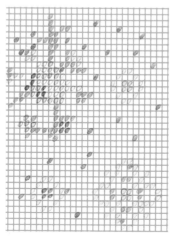

*Pattern for small purse.*

## MATERIALS FOR LARGE PURSE

*2 pieces of double-thread 18-
gauge canvas, each 9in (22cm)
× 7in (18cm)*
*16in (40cm) × 3in (8cm) double-
thread 18-gauge canvas*
*2 pieces of pale gray fabric, each*

*7in (17cm) × 5in (13cm)*
*1 piece of the same fabric
measuring 14in (35cm) × 2in
(5cm)*
*Matching sewing thread*
*Tapestry needle size 24*

### Threads

*Susan Bates Anchor stranded
cotton*
*2 skeins of each of the following
colors:*
**pale gray** *398;* **peach** *8;* **pale
green** *203;* **beige** *852*
*1 skein of each of the following
colors:*

**green** *214, 227, 258;* **blue** *118;*
**dark peach** *9;* **pink** *778, 868;*
**ecru**

### Embroidery Stitches

*Tent stitch, herringbone stitch,
back stitch.*

## DIRECTIONS

▦  Run a vertical and a horizontal
line of guide basting through the
centers of the rectangles, taking
care not to cross any threads
running the opposite way. Match
these to the corresponding lines
on the diagram to find the center
of the design.

▦  Working from the center
outwards embroider the design in
tent stitch following the picture
carefully.

▦  To make the gusset: work a
strip of tent stitch nine stitches
wide and approximately 13in

(33cm) long, using the pale gray
thread. When the embroidery is
completed, block it carefully (see
page 79), making sure that the
front and back pieces are exactly
the same size.

▦  Trim away the surplus canvas
round each piece of embroidery
leaving a margin of ⅜in (1cm).

▦  Using back stitch and the pale
gray thread, join one edge of the
gusset to the front piece and then
the other edge of the gusset to
the back piece.

▦  Turn over the ⅜in (1cm) margin
round the top of the bag and
secure with a row of herringbone
stitch.

▦  Cut out the lining ⅜in (1cm)
larger than the finished
embroidered front, back and
gusset and join the seams. Turn
and press a ⅜in (1cm) hem round
the top of the lining.

▦  Make a twisted cord
approximately 1yd (1m) long from
10 lengths of stranded cotton.
Decorate it with a tassel as
shown in the photograph and
sew each end of the cord
securely to the inside of the
gusset on the bag.

▦  Slipstitch the lining in place.

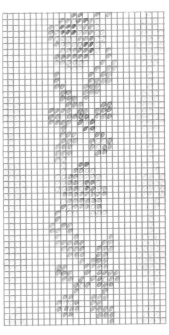

*Pattern for large purse.*

# FINISHING OFF

## PRESSING

Embroidery on fabric will need a light pressing to smooth out any wrinkles in the fabric caused by the stitching.

▣ Before pressing, pad the ironing board with a thick, folded towel and lay the embroidery over it face down.

▣ Cover the embroidery with a damp piece of thin cotton fabric and press lightly, letting the iron just touch the pressing cloth. Take care not to crush heavily stitched areas. Let the embroidery dry thoroughly.

## MITERING CORNERS ON FABRIC

This method of finishing corners on a piece of fabric will ensure a neat, crisp finish.

▣ Fold over a narrow hem along each edge of the fabric and press. Trim the corner to reduce bulk, turn over the corner and press.

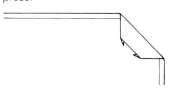

▣ Fold over the two sides as shown and pin in place. Hand or machine stitch along the hem. Hand stitch the diagonal joining if the hem is quite wide.

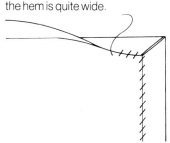

## MITERING CORNERS ON CANVAS

This way of finishing corners on canvas work will give a neat edge without bulk. Always block the canvas before finishing the edges.

▣ Trim the corner of the surplus canvas to reduce the bulk.

▣ Turn over the canvas to the corner of the embroidery.

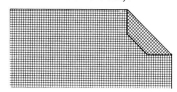

▣ Fold in the side edges, making sure that the corner is square, and tack in place. Then secure the edge and the mitered corner with a row of hand stitching.

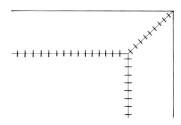

## BLOCKING

Canvas work should be blocked to straighten the grain of the canvas, which becomes distorted during the stitching, even when an embroidery frame has been used. For blocking: you will need a piece of wood or blockboard larger than the embroidery and covered with a sheet of clean polythene; rustproof tacks; a hammer; a steel rule or tapemeasure; a water spray or sponge.

▣ If the canvas has a selvadge, cut small nicks along it to ensure that it stretches evenly.

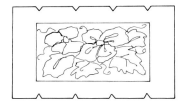

▣ Damp the canvas work with the spray or a wet sponge and place it face down on the board. Lightly hammer tacks at center top and bottom of the surplus canvas, stretching the canvas gently downwards. Repeat this at each side, checking that the warp and weft threads of the canvas are at right angles to each other.

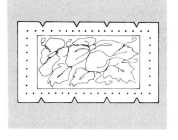

▣ Working outwards from the center of each side, insert more tacks at ¾in (2cm) intervals, stretching the canvas gently as you proceed.

▣ Check the size and shape of the canvas to make sure the stretching is even and adjust the tacks where necessary. Hammer all the tacks in securely. Spray or sponge the canvas so that it is evenly damp all over and leave it to dry at room temperature for several days. A second blocking may be needed to straighten strongly vertical or horizontal designs.

## CUSHION COVER

This cushion cover is made quite simply from one folded piece of fabric without fastenings.

▣ Finish the short edges of the fabric by turning a narrow hem and machine stitching.

▣ Fold the fabric as shown, making sure that the narrow flap is on top. Pin the sides.

▣ Machine stitch along either side of the cushion cover stitching across the fabric folds which will form a flap.

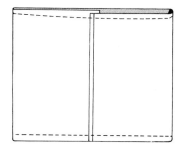

▣ Turn the cushion cover right side out, gently pushing the corners out fully. Press well.

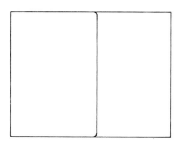

| Page | Acknowledgments (Photographer/Stylist) |
|---|---|
| 9 | Marcel Duffas/Isabelle Garçon |
| 13 | Elizabeth Novick/Isabelle Garçon |
| 15 | Marcel Duffas/Isabelle Garçon |
| 16,17 | Bernard Maltaverne/Caroline Lebeau |
| 18,19 | Jérome Tisné/Isabelle Garçon |
| 22,23 | Marcel Duffas/Janick Schoumacher |
| 25 | Marcel Duffas/Isabelle Garçon |
| 28,29 | Jean Pierre Godeaut/Marion Faver |
| 31,32,33 | Alex Bianchi/Isabelle Garçon |
| 35,36 | Marcel Duffas/Janick Schoumacher |
| 39,40,41 | Gilles de Chabaneix/Isabelle Garçon |
| 43 | Gilles de Chabaneix/Caroline Lebeau |
| 44,45 | Alex Bianchi/Isabelle Garçon |
| 48 | Nicolas Bruant/Caroline Lebeau |
| 50,51 | Jérôme Tisné/Isabelle Garçon |
| 52,53 | Marcel Duffas/Isabelle Garçon |
| 56,57 | Bernard Maltaverne/Caroline Lebeau |
| 58,59 | Yves Duronsoy/Andrée Jacobs |
| 61,63 | Marcel Duffas/Isabelle Garçon |
| 65,66,67,68 | Bernard Maltaverne/Caroline Lebeau |
| 69 | Marcel Duffas/Isabelle Garçon |
| 73 | Bernard Maltaverne/Marion Faver |
| 77,78 | Joël Laiter/Isabelle Garçon |